The Contented
Little Baby Book

The Contented Little Baby Book

*The Simple Secrets of Calm,
Confident Parenting*

GINA FORD

NEW AMERICAN LIBRARY

New American Library
Published by New American Library, a division of Penguin Group (USA) Inc.,
375 Hudson Street, New York, New York 10014, USA
Penguin Group (Canada), 90 Eglinton Avenue East, Suite 700, Toronto, Ontario M4P 2Y3,
Canada (a division of Pearson Penguin Canada Inc.)
Penguin Books Ltd., 80 Strand, London WC2R 0RL, England
Penguin Ireland, 25 St. Stephen's Green, Dublin 2, Ireland
(a division of Penguin Books Ltd.)
Penguin Group (Australia), 250 Camberwell Road, Camberwell,
Victoria 3124, Australia (a division of Pearson Australia Group Pty. Ltd.)
Penguin Books India Pvt. Ltd., 11 Community Centre, Panchsheel Park,
New Delhi - 110 017, India
Penguin Group (NZ), cnr Airborne and Rosedale Roads, Albany,
Auckland 1310, New Zealand (a division of Pearson New Zealand Ltd.)
Penguin Books (South Africa) (Pty.) Ltd., 24 Sturdee Avenue, Rosebank, Johannesburg 2196,
South Africa

Penguin Books Ltd., Registered Offices:
80 Strand, London WC2R 0RL, England

Published by New American Library, a division of Penguin Group (USA) Inc. Originally
published in a different form in Great Britain by Vermilion, an imprint of Ebury Press.

First New American Library Printing, October 2001
10 9

N
A
L   REGISTERED TRADEMARK—MARCA REGISTRADA

LIBRARY OF CONGRESS CATALOGING-IN-PUBLICATION DATA:

Ford, Gina.
    The contented little baby book : the simple secrets of calm, confident parenting / Gina Ford.
        p.   cm.
    Includes index.
    ISBN 0-451-20243-0
    1. Infants—Care. 2. Infants—Health and hygiene. 3. Parenting. 4. Child rearing. I. Title.
RJ131 .F64 2001
649'.1—dc21   00-048185

Set in Times New Roman

Printed in the United States of America   ·

PUBLISHER'S NOTE
The information contained here is not intended to replace the advice that you should
receive from your doctor or other health professional. Every infant is different, and varia-
tions in care may be recommended based on individual circumstances.

To my beloved mother and best friend
in blessed remembrance of all her wisdom, the very special love,
support and encouragement she always gave me
and whose wonderful smile and sparkling eyes
could turn a rainy day into sunshine.

CONTENTS

ACKNOWLEDGMENTS

I would like to thank the Hodgsons for their wonderful friendship and constant support: Keith, for his invaluable help in transforming my Routines and Feeding Plans into at-a-glance form, so making easier reading for parents; and Janetta, for her endless patience and the late nights she spent helping transform my often very rough drafts into an understandable and readable manuscript for my editor Joanna Carreras. I thank Joanna for being so supportive and patient during the writing of this book and for all her excellent editorial changes and ideas.

A special debt of thanks to my dear cousin Sheila Eskdale and special friends Jane Revell and Joanne Amps. Their endless phone calls and notes of encouragement has given me enormous emotional support.

Finally, I would like to thank the hundreds of parents all over the world who have shared their babies with me. Without their experiences and continual feedback over the years, this book would not have been possible.

Gina Ford
February 2001

INTRODUCTION

Most of the books about small babies on the market at present are written by doctors, psychologists or people of that status. Their information is based on their own children, or parents and children who have participated in research studies. While the medical information and developmental text can be interesting, one would have to question how much help it can be to the average first-time mother getting to grips with the never-ending demands of a new baby.

For instance, most of the books will inform you that it is normal for a baby to wake up several times a night, and that you should feed on demand as often and for as long as your baby wants, and allow the baby to find his own sleep pattern. For the authors of these books, this approach does not necessarily present a problem, as their work can probably be done at any time of the day to fit in with the baby sleeping. But what about the parents who have to get up at 7:00 A.M. to deal with older children or start a day's work around 9:00 A.M.? After a few weeks, these continual wakings can reduce even the sanest of human beings into complete wrecks. You will be told that things will get better, yet recent surveys show that 85 percent of children are still waking up at night by the age of one year. The baby experts have no answer; many of them experience the same sleepless-nights syndrome themselves, but they probably do not suffer as much as other parents who are dictated to by a strict schedule and heavy workloads.

Baby business is big business. Look at the shelves of any good book-shop; you will find literally dozens and dozens of baby books. Flick through the pages dealing with sleep and feeding, and you will find the advice is nearly always the same: "Rock your baby, walk the floor, nurse him to sleep on the breast, put him in a sling or drive him around the block in the car." Every day thousands of parents are doing all of these things, some for months, others for years. They then go on to the second stage of reading: "How to solve your children's sleep problems." In these books you are told that the reason your baby has a sleep problem is that he has learned the wrong associations: i.e. rocking, feeding to induce sleep, driving around the block to induce sleep. Their solution to the problem, if you are strong enough, is to use the controlled crying method, which basically means letting your baby cry himself to sleep. This can sometimes take up to two hours over several nights before he learns to go to sleep on his own.

Well, why can't we just leave them to cry when they are tiny, so they learn from day one to settle themselves to sleep? The answer to that, according to yet another few shelves of books, is that leaving your baby to cry could psychologically disturb him for life. As I have already said, books are "big business," lots of theory and very few answers, so that you have to go out and buy the next one.

What is so different about my book is that it comes from years of hands-on experience. I have lived with and cared for hundreds of different babies. I offer real and practical advice on how to establish a good feeding and sleeping pattern from day one, thus avoiding months of sleepless nights, colic, feeding difficulties, and many of the other problems that the experts convince us are a normal part of parenting.

The routines will teach you to recognize the difference between hunger and tiredness and how to meet all your baby's needs, which will result in a very happy, contented baby, who is likely to sleep through the night at around six to ten weeks. My advice will teach you how to listen to what your baby is really saying. It has worked for hundreds of mothers and their babies all over the world; it can work for you too.

Finally, for no particular reason, and I hope this does not cause offense, the mother is always "she," the father is always "he" and the baby is always "he."

❀ 1 ❀

Preparation for the birth

When one talks of preparing for the birth, the first things that spring to mind are prenatal care and decorating the nursery. Both are important in their own ways. Prenatal care is of the utmost importance for a healthy pregnancy and essential to prepare you for the birth, and decorating the nursery for the new arrival is fun. While many of the classes do give some advice on what is ahead after the birth, they often overlook very practical tips, which if offered early enough, could save the parents hours of time and stress after the baby is born.

If you follow my routines from day one, you should be fortunate enough to have a content and happy baby with some time for yourself. However, as you will see from my routines and charts, spare time is extremely limited (and, believe me, mothers who are not following a routine have even less spare time). In this short amount of time, unless you have hired help, you will have to fit in the cooking of meals, shopping, laundry, etc.

By doing the following things before the baby is born you will gain many hours of free time after the birth:

- Order all your nursery equipment well in advance. Cribs can sometimes take up to 12 weeks to be delivered, and there are many advantages in having the big crib from the beginning. (See page 3.)
- Have all the bed linen, washcloths and towels washed and ready

for use. Make up the crib, bassinet and stroller. Prepare everything in the nursery so it is at hand the minute you get home from the hospital.

- Have all the baby essentials in stock: cotton balls, baby oil, diapers, diaper rash and moisturizing creams, baby wipes, soft sponges, baby brush, baby wash and baby shampoo.
- Check that all the electrical equipment is working properly. Learn how the sterilizer works and how to put together the feeding bottles.
- Arrange a section of counter space in the kitchen where preparation and sterilizing can be done. Ideally it should be directly below a cupboard where all the baby's feeding equipment can be stored.
- Stock up on soap powder, cleaning materials and enough paper towels and toilet paper to last at least six weeks.
- Prepare and freeze a large selection of healthy homemade meals. If you are breast feeding you should avoid the frozen dinners that are full of additives and preservatives.
- Stock up on extra dry goods such as tea, coffee, snacks, etc; it is inevitable that you will have extra visitors the first month, and supplies will soon go down.
- Purchase birthday gifts and cards for any upcoming birthdays. Also have a good selection of thank-you cards ready to send for all the gifts you will receive.
- Get up-to-date with any odd jobs that need to be done in the house or garden. The last thing you need once the baby has arrived is the hassle of repairmen coming and going.
- If breast-feeding, book your electric breast pump well in advance; they are in big demand!

The nursery

Like most parents, you will most probably have your baby sleeping in your room with you during the night. However, I can't stress enough the importance of having the nursery ready on your return from the hospital. All too often a mother will call me in a complete panic asking for advice on how to get a three-month-old baby used to their own room. Many tears and much anxiety could have been avoided if the mother had got the baby used to his own room from day one. Instead, for the first few weeks the baby dozes on and off during the early part of the evening in a car seat, then is taken to the parents' room for the last feed and the night. It is not surprising that these babies feel very abandoned when they are eventually put to sleep by themselves, in an unfamiliar dark room.

From the very beginning you should use the nursery for diaper changing and naps. In the evening after the bath, feed and settle the baby there from 7:00 P.M. to 10:00 P.M. The baby can still be transferred to your room after the last feed, to make middle-of-the-night feeding easier. But by getting your baby used to his room from the beginning, he will very quickly enjoy being there and see it as a peaceful haven, not a prison.

When my babies are very small, if they have become overtired or overstimulated, I find that they will calm down immediately when taken to their room. And by six weeks they are positively beaming when taken to their nursery for the bath and bedtime routine.

Decoration and furnishings

It is not essential to spend a fortune on decorating and furnishing the baby's room. A room with walls, windows and bedsheets covered in teddy bears soon becomes very boring. Plain walls can easily be brightened up with a colorful border, and perhaps a matching valance and tiebacks; this makes it easy to adapt the room as the baby grows, but avoids the need to redecorate totally. (Another very cost-effective and fun way to liven up the room is to use sheets of children's wrapping paper as posters, which are bright and colorful—and can be changed frequently.)

The following guidelines should be observed when choosing furnishings and fittings for the nursery.

The crib

Most baby books advise that in the early days a crib is not necessary, as babies are happier in a bassinet or small crib. I am not convinced they are happier and sleep better in these. As I have mentioned earlier, I much prefer to get my babies used to their big crib from day one. By doing this I have never encountered a problem when they outgrow the bassinet and start to sleep the whole night in their big crib in the nursery.

When choosing a crib, it is important to remember that it will be your baby's bed for at least two or three years, and it should be sturdy enough to withstand a bouncing toddler. Even very young babies will eventually move around their crib.

Choose a design without fancy posts or decorative cutouts that could be quite painful for a young baby. Crib bumpers are not advised for babies under one year old, as they often end up sleeping with their heads pressed up against the bumpers. Because body heat escapes through the top of the head, blocking this off causes the risk of overheating, which is thought to be a contributing cause of SIDS.

The other points to look for when choosing a crib are:

- Choose one with two or three different base height levels.
- Drop sides should be easy to put up and down without making a noise. Test several times.
- It should be large enough to accommodate a two-year-old child comfortably.
- All cribs must comply with the recommendations set out by the U.S. Consumer Product Safety Commission. Slats should be no wider than $2\frac{3}{8}$ inches apart, while corner posts can protrude no more than $\frac{1}{16}$ of an inch above the end panels. There should be at least 9 inches between the mattress and top of the crib.
- Buy the best possible mattress that you can afford. I have found that foam mattresses tend to sink in the middle within a few months. The mattress must fit snugly, with no more than two finger widths between it and the crib side. All mattresses must comply with Standards of the U.S. Consumer Product Safety Commission.

Bedding required for the crib

Everything should be 100 percent cotton so that it can be washed in hot water along with the baby's night clothes. Due to the risk of the baby overheating or smothering, quilts and duvets are not recommended for babies under one year old. If you want a pretty matching top cover for your baby's cot, make sure it is 100 percent cotton and not quilted with a nylon filling. For parents who are handy with a sewing machine, a considerable amount of money can be saved by making flat sheets and draw sheets out of a large cotton double-bed sheet.

You will need a minimum of the following bedding:

- Three stretch cotton fitted bottom sheets. Choose the soft jersey-type cotton rather than the toweling type, which very quickly can become rough and worn-looking.
- Six flat, smooth cotton top sheets. Avoid flannel, which gives off too much fluff for young babies; this can obstruct the nose and cause breathing problems. Folded in half, these sheets are also ideal as draw sheets, which you put across the head end of the bottom sheet. They can be easily replaced in the middle of the night, thus eliminating the need to remake the whole crib should your baby leak or dribble.
- Three cotton, small-weave cellular blankets, plus one warmer blanket for very cold nights.

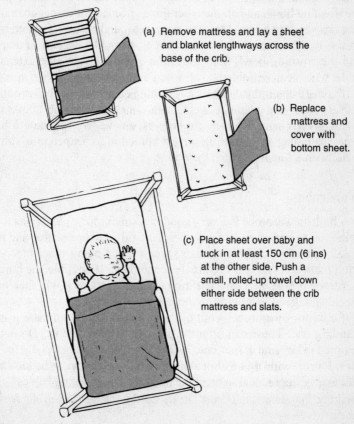

(a) Remove mattress and lay a sheet and blanket lengthways across the base of the crib.

(b) Replace mattress and cover with bottom sheet.

(c) Place sheet over baby and tuck in at least 150 cm (6 ins) at the other side. Push a small, rolled-up towel down either side between the crib mattress and slats.

Making up the crib

Changing station

There are special units designed as changing stations that have the changing mat placed on the top and two shelves below for diapers and all the other equipment needed. Again, like so much of the other specially designed baby equipment, they are not really practical. The main reasons are that the top is never large enough to include a washing bowl for sponge baths so a further table is required at the side. It is also difficult to access items stored at the back of the shelves below, which are difficult to keep neat and tidy due to their depth.

By far the best type of changing station I have used is a long unit consisting of drawers and a cupboard. The top is long enough to hold the changing mat and still leaves enough room at the bottom end to place the washing bowl, and all the other things needed for diaper changing. The drawers can be used to store sleepwear, underwear, bibs and burp cloths, and the cupboard will hold larger items like packets of diapers and the washing bowl. Sometimes these units have a side extension table, which can be folded down when not in use, thus saving space.

If you are determined to have everything coordinated, I believe some nursery furniture manufacturers have a design like the above that matches their crib, but they are very expensive. By spending a little time searching, it is possible to get something cheaper in a similar style, with a finish to match the crib.

Wardrobe

A built-in wardrobe is a very good investment for a nursery as it enables you to keep the baby's clothes neat, tidy and crease free and provides you with valuable storage space for the many other pieces of equipment that you will eventually accumulate. If possible, the built-in wardrobe is best built on a partition or a hall wall, as it will then have the advantage of helping to soundproof the nursery.

If a built-in wardrobe is out of the question, try to purchase a freestanding one. These can often be picked up very cheaply. Do not be tempted to buy one of the "cute" wardrobes designed especially for babies; I have found that within a few months, they prove to be too small and totally impractical to meet the needs of fast-growing babies.

Chair

It is essential, no matter how small your baby's room is, that you try to fit in a chair. The ideal chair could also be used as a breast-feeding chair, so it should have a straight back, be wide enough to allow room for both you and your baby as he grows and have arms to support you while breast-feeding. Later on it will support you as you hold your toddler while reading the bedtime story. Many parents are attracted to a rocking chair, but these can prove to be quite dangerous as your baby becomes more mobile and attempts to pull himself up holding on to the chair. In the early days it can also be tempting to settle the baby by rocking him to sleep, but this is one of the main causes of a baby developing poor sleeping habits.

Curtains

Curtains should be full length and fully lined. It is of the utmost importance that they are fixed to a track that fits flush along the top of the window. Ideally they should have a deep matching valance, which is also lined. There should be no gaps between the sides of the curtains and the window frame; even the smallest chink of light can be enough to wake your baby earlier than 7:00 A.M. For the same reason, curtain rods should be avoided as the light streams out of the gap at the top. As the baby gets older, he may not settle back to sleep if woken at 5:00 A.M. by early morning sun or streetlights.*

I am so convinced that a dark room encourages good sleeping habits that I will not take a booking unless the nursery has both curtains with blackout lining and a special blackout shade (see Useful addresses). When the lights are off and the curtains closed, it should be so dark that you are unable to see your partner standing at the other side of the room. Research has also proved that the chemicals in the brain alter in the dark, conditioning it for sleep. This is one of the reasons why, in the early days, I put my babies in a dark room for all their naps.

---

* Editor's Note: Blackout linings and shades are available in the United States from Hunter Douglas. See www.nobrainerblinds.com.

Alexander: aged three years

Alexander was three years old when I went to care for his newborn sister. As a baby he was fed on demand, and on the advice of the maternity nurse was left to find his own sleep pattern. By nine months of age Alexander was still waking up several times a night and his parents were so exhausted and desperate for sleep that they decided to try the Richard Ferber sleep training method (see Further reading). *Over a period of one week, when he woke up in the night he was left to settle himself back to sleep; his parents would check him, but not talk to him. They gradually extended the checking time until they were not going in at all. By the end of the week, he was sleeping through from 7:00 P.M. to 5:00 A.M., but once awake he was ready to begin the day. The parents accepted this early start to the day; after nine months of being woken several times a night they were just grateful that he actually slept a solid ten hours.*

However, when they had their second baby, they realized that Alexander's very early start and caring for a newborn baby would be very difficult. I suggested that they try putting him to bed later to see if he would sleep later, but they had tried this on many occasions and he would still wake at 5:00 A.M.

They had also tried leaving him to cry, but this was quite difficult as he nearly always woke up yelling, "I've done a poo." If left for any length of time, he would attempt to change his own diaper, which turned out to be a very messy business!

I observed Alexander for several days. Because of his early start he was exhausted by 11:00 A.M. and needed to go down for a nap; sometimes this nap would last two hours. I suggested they cut the nap back to a strict 45 minutes, as if left longer than this he would go back into a deep sleep and be very difficult to wake. I was also concerned about his diet; obviously something was triggering his bowels to work very early in the morning. I advised that he be given his main protein meal at lunchtime, and stick to a carbohydrate supper. Also the amount of fruit and dried fruit he consumed in the day concerned me, especially in the afternoon, so we made sure that he had most of his daily intake of fruit and dried fruit before 3:00 P.M. The change in diet certainly worked regarding his bowel movements, as he stopped doing a poo at 5:00 A.M., but unfortunately he kept waking up.

I then realized that every time we went in to him at 5:00 A.M. he was standing at the window, which had no curtains and only a shade. Although it was a dense shade, as with all of this type of window treatment, the light shone out from the top and down the sides. I was convinced that this was the main reason he would not settle himself back to sleep. It was harder to convince his parents. However, the bedroom his baby sister occupied was fitted with a blackout blind and blackout lined curtains, and at one month she slept through the night from her last feed and had to be woken at 7:00 A.M. every morning. This helped persuade Alexander's parents of the importance of a totally dark room, and we fitted the window with full-length curtains and a deep box valance, both lined with blackout fabric.

Now when Alexander woke up, it was so dark he could no longer see his way to the window. I would go straight to him when he cried out and repeat the same words, no matter how many times I had to go in to him. I would say "It's not morning yet; be a good boy and go back to sleep, until Daddy comes for you." I would not get into a conversation with him; whatever he said I would just repeat the same words. Within one week he was still waking up at 5:00 A.M., but very quickly going back to sleep until 7:00 A.M. By the end of two weeks he was going from 7:00 P.M. to 7:30 A.M. every night. A year later he continues to sleep until 7:00 to 7:30 A.M., and I am convinced that the main problem here was light. All babies and young children will come into a light sleep or wake between 5:00 A.M. to 6:00 A.M., but if a room is dark enough, they will be much more likely to go back to sleep.

Alexander's sister, now aged 15 months, despite two colds and several trips abroad, has never woken up before 7:00 A.M. When the family travels, the first thing they pack is two lengths of attachable blackout linings!

Carpeting

A fully fitted carpet is preferable to rugs, which can be a potential danger for tripping on when you are attending to your baby in the dim light. Choose a carpet that is treated with a stain-guard and avoid very dark or bright colors, as they tend to show the dirt more easily.

Lighting

If the main light is not already fitted with a dimmer switch, it would be worthwhile to change it. In the early days, dimming the lights when settling the baby is a good association signal. If you are on a limited budget, purchase one of the small plug-in night-lights that fit into any normal 13-amp electrical socket. I always use one of these lights in the middle of the night, regardless of whether a dimmer switch is fitted.

Baby equipment

Bassinet or small crib

As I mentioned earlier, a bassinet is not really essential. Even the cheapest bassinet and stand can cost over $50, which is quite a lot of money for something unessential that your baby will outgrow within six weeks. However, if you live in a very large house or plan to travel in the first few weeks, it may be useful. If your budget is limited, try to borrow one from a friend and buy a new mattress.

It's also possible to buy smaller versions of a regular-sized crib. Certainly they are much longer than a bassinet, but not really any more practical. Because we now put our babies to sleep on their backs, these narrow cribs create a problem for small babies. They wake themselves up several times a night because the cribs are not wide enough for them to sleep with their arms stretched out fully, and they get their hands caught between the spars.

If you do decide to use either of the above for a short period, you will need the following bedding:

- Three fitted, stretch cotton bottom sheets. Choose the soft, smooth jersey-type cotton.
- Six smooth cotton flat crib sheets, to be used as top sheets and later as sheets on the big crib.
- Four cotton, cellular close-weave blankets.
- A dozen diaper cloths to be placed across the top of the bassinet or crib to catch dribbles.

Baby carriage

The traditional carriage is very expensive and not really appropriate to modern-day living. Most parents find it more practical to choose one of the other smaller types of transport available now. When choosing a carriage or stroller, it is important to take into consideration where you live and your lifestyle. For example, if you have to drive to the nearest stores, it is important to choose a simple, portable stroller that is easy to put up and down and not too heavy for constant lifting in and out of the car trunk. There are now some very lightweight strollers on the market that recline flat for a newborn baby, and come with a hood to give the baby some protection in cold weather.

If you are likely to be using your stroller in a town area, or in stores with narrow spaces (e.g. aisles in supermarkets), swivel wheels are a godsend. They make turning the stroller around corners effortless compared to those with set wheels.

Whatever type you choose, you should practice putting it up and down several times, and try lifting it onto a surface in the shop to get an idea of how easy it is going to be to lift into the trunk.

The following guidelines should also be observed when purchasing a carriage or stroller:

- It should be fitted with good strong safety straps that go around the waist, and have an easy-to-operate brake. Make sure it has a hood and apron to protect the baby in colder weather.
- Buy all the extras at the same time: sun canopy, rain cover, head support cushion and storage area. Models often change in design and sometimes dimension, and if you wait till the following season, the items you require might not fit or match.
- Try pushing it around the shop to check if the handle height is a comfortable level; also observe how easy it is to get in and out of doorways and around corners.

Car seat

A car seat should always be used, even for the shortest journeys. Never be tempted to travel holding your baby in your arms. It's against the law! If the car had to stop suddenly or, even worse, was in a collision, tests have proved that it is impossible to keep hold of the baby. It is also dangerous to put the baby's car seat on the front seat of a car fitted with air bags. Some seats come with adjustable backs and a rocking mode so that they can double up as a seat in the house. As with the crib, choose the best you can afford and one that comes with very clear instructions on how to install the seat.* Things to look for when choosing a car seat are:

- A seat with large side wings that will give your baby more head protection from a side-on impact collision.
- A car seat fitted with a one-pull harness will make it much easier to adjust to suit the needs of your baby's clothing.
- The buckle should be easy to open and close, but not easy enough for a child to open.
- Look for extra accessories like a sunshade, head support pillow and replacement cover.
- Follow the latest safety regulations recommended by your pediatrician.

Baby bath

A baby bath is another item that is not essential. Like the bassinet, babies outgrow the small bath very quickly. A newborn baby can be bathed in a hand basin to begin with, or even a big bathtub, using one of the several types of bath seats that are available for tiny babies. These allow the baby to lie, supported and on a slight slope, leaving the mother with both hands free to wash the baby.

If you would feel more confident with a special baby bath, the one I would recommend is designed to fit across a big bathtub. It makes filling and emptying much easier, unlike the traditional baby bath that sits on a stand, and has to be filled and emptied using a bucket.

Another design is a bath that is incorporated in a changing station. I have found these totally impractical because as you lift the baby out of the bath, you have to maneuver the lid, which doubles as the changing table, down over the top of the bath before you can put the baby on it to dry and dress him. They are also very difficult to empty; I found I always had to tip the whole thing on its side to drain the water out com-

---

* Because there are many types of car seats, vehicle seats and safety belts, be sure to follow the car seat manufacturer's instructions as well as your vehicle owner's manual for proper installation. When the car seat is installed, be sure it can't move side to side or toward the front of the car.

pletely. This usually ended up with all the items stored below toppling out onto the floor. These bath/changing stations are very expensive, and I would discourage anyone from buying them.

Changing mat

It is worthwhile buying two changing mats and keeping the spare one downstairs. Choose them in plastic for easy cleaning. In the early days it is best to lay a hand towel on the top, as very young babies hate to be laid down on anything cold.

Baby monitor

This is another piece of equipment on which I would not advise skimping. There are two types to choose from: plug-in and mobile, and I always advise parents to go for the mobile one. They usually have a clip that can be attached to a pocket or belt, allowing you to move freely around the house. This is very useful if you want to take a bath or go to the garage, places that often do not have an electrical outlet. Most have a sound-activated visual light display that allows you to turn the volume down but still monitor whether the baby is crying or not. The one with the best sound quality, and the most portable that I have used, is a rechargeable one, which has a very small portable unit within the parent unit. It is the most expensive on the market, but well worth the extra money.

When choosing a baby monitor, look for the following:

- Monitors work using radio frequencies, so choose a model with two channels, allowing you to switch channels if there is interference.
- A rechargeable model is more expensive initially, but the saving on batteries will make it cheaper in the long run.
- A low-battery indicator and an out-of-range indicator.

Baby sling

Some parents swear by this method of moving around with their babies. I never use one, as I find it too big a strain on my back to carry a baby around like this for any length of time.

Very small babies are also inclined to go straight to sleep the minute you hold them close to your chest, which defeats the whole purpose of my routines, i.e. keeping the baby awake at certain times of the day, and teaching the baby the right associations of going to sleep on his own. I do think that as babies get bigger, slings are a very useful way for parents to carry them around, especially when the baby is old enough to face forward.

If you feel a sling would be useful, the following guidelines should be observed when choosing one:

- It should have safety tabs to ensure that it cannot come undone.
- It must provide your baby with enough head and neck support; some come with a detachable cushion that gives extra support for very young babies.
- It should offer the choice of the baby facing in or outward, and have a seat with an adjustable height position.
- It should be made of a strong washable fabric, with comfortable padded shoulder straps.

Baby chair

While many parents use the car seat in the house for the baby to sit in during the day, if your budget will stretch to it, a second seat can be a great bonus as it saves having to move the same seat from room to room.

A baby seat is designed differently from a car seat. The rigid type will have adjustable seat positions and a base that can either remain stable or be changed to a rocking mode. These chairs can also be used for your baby to sit in during the early stages of weaning.

Another type of seat available is called a "bouncy chair." This is a very lightweight seat made up of a steel frame covered in fabric and is designed to bounce as the baby moves. I have found them very popular with babies over two months, but they can be frightening to some tiny babies. Whatever type of chair you choose, make sure your baby, no matter how tiny, is securely strapped in and never leave him unsupervised in either type of chair. Finally, always place your baby on the floor when he is in his seat; never be tempted to leave him on a table or work top.

Whichever type you decide to buy, observe the following guidelines:

- The frame and base should be firm and sturdy, and be fitted with a strong safety strap.

- Choose one with an easily removable and washable cover.
- Purchase a head support cushion for tiny babies.

Playpen

Nowadays playpens are often frowned upon, as some "baby experts" feel they hinder the baby's natural instinct to explore. While no baby should be left for long periods in a playpen, they can be very useful for ensuring that your child is safe when you are preparing lunch or need to go to the bathroom or answer the door. If you decide to use a playpen, get your baby used to it from a very young age.

Some parents use portable playpens, but if you have the space, I recommend a sturdy play yard, which is much larger and enables the baby to pull himself up easily and to walk around. Whichever type you choose, make sure that it is situated out of reach of radiators, curtains, etc; and never hang toys on pieces of string in the playpen, as this could be fatal if your baby got tangled up in the string. Babies have been known to strangle themselves this way.

Important points to look for when choosing a playpen are:

- Make sure it has a fixed floor so that the baby cannot move it.
- Check that there are no sharp metal hinges or catches on which your baby can harm himself.
- If choosing a mesh-type playpen, make sure that the mesh is strong enough to prevent your baby pushing small toys through and making a hole big enough to trap his hand or fingers.

Equipment needed for breast-feeding

Nursing bra

These are bras made with specially designed cups that can either be unhooked or unzipped, making breast-feeding easier. It is important that you choose a well-fitting bra with wide adjustable shoulder straps to help support your breasts. The bra should not press tightly against the nipples, as this can cause blocked milk ducts. As you will need to wear your bra day and night, you may find cotton ones preferable to polyester. Buy two before the birth, and once your milk has come in, if they prove to be comfortable, you'll want to purchase two more.

Breast pads

In the early days you will use lots of disposable breast pads, as they will need to be changed every time your baby feeds and, if your breasts fill up quickly, sometimes in between feeds. Most of my mothers prefer the round ones, contoured to fit the breasts. The more expensive brands usually work out cheaper in the long run, as they are normally more absorbent. Buy one box at first, and if that brand is suitable, you can then stock up with them.

Nursing pillow

Nursing pillows, also known as "boppy pillows," are shaped to fit around a mother's waist, bringing small babies up to the perfect height for breast-feeding. They can also be used for propping babies up, and make an excellent back support for older babies who are learning to sit up. Make sure you choose one with a removable, machine-washable cover.

Nipple creams and sprays

These creams and sprays are supposed to help care for the breasts and relieve them of any pain caused by breast-feeding. As discussed in the breast-feeding section, poor positioning of the baby on the breast is usually the main cause of pain. If you experience pain when you are feeding your baby, it would be wise to consult your doctor or breast-feeding consultant before using a cream or spray. She will check that you are positioning the baby on the breast correctly, and advise on which cream or spray, if any, should be used. No other special creams or soaps are recommended when breast-feeding. Wash your breasts twice a day with plain water, and after each feed the nipples should be rubbed with a little breast milk and allowed to air dry.

Electric breast pump

I am convinced that one of the reasons the majority of my mothers are so successful at breast-feeding is because I encourage the use of an electric breast pump. In the very early days when the mothers are producing more milk than their baby needs (especially first thing in the morning), I get them to express from the second breast, using one of these very powerful breast pumps. The expressed milk is then stored in the fridge or freezer and can be used as a top-up later in the day when sometimes the mother's milk supply is low. This, I believe, is one of the main reasons why so many babies are restless and will not settle after their bath in the evening. The other advantage of expressing in the early days is when the baby goes through a growth spurt, the mother simply expresses less, immediately providing the baby with the extra milk he needs. This avoids her going back to demand feeding for several days in order to increase her milk supply, which is the usual advice given for increasing the milk supply during growth spurts.

If you want to breast-feed and quickly establish your baby in a routine, an electric breast pump will be a big asset. Do not be persuaded to go for one of the smaller hand versions; they are much slower at drawing the milk off, which is one reason why so many women give up expressing. When ordering your breast pump, it is worthwhile buying an additional one that includes extra bottles and caps, which will save you the worry of always having to sterilize.

For information about where to hire a breast pump, see Useful addresses at the end of this book.

Freezer bags

Expressed milk can be stored in the fridge for up to 24 hours, or in the freezer for one month. These specially designed presterilized bags are an ideal way to store expressed breast milk and are available from most drugstores and baby departments in the larger stores.

Feeding bottles

Most breast-feeding consultants are totally against newborn babies being given a bottle, even of expressed milk. They claim that it creates nipple confusion and reduces the baby's desire to suck on the mother's breast, which leads to a poor milk supply and the mother giving up breast-feeding altogether. My own view is that the majority of women give up breast-feeding because they are totally exhausted by "demand feeding," often several times a night. From the first week all my babies are introduced to a bottle of either expressed milk or formula milk; this one bottle a day is given either last thing in the evening or during the night. This allows my mothers to sleep for several hours at a stretch, so they are much more able to cope with breast-feeding. I have never had the problem of a baby rejecting the mother's breast, or becoming confused between the nipple and the teat. However, I do believe that this could happen if in the early days a baby was allowed more than one bottle a day.

A problem about which I receive a considerable number of telephone calls is the one of "older babies" refusing a bottle. These babies have been breast-fed exclusively, usually for three or four months. The mother is often returning to work, and finds that her baby absolutely refuses the bottle. This can lead to an enormous battle and weeks of struggling to get him to take a bottle—another good reason for getting your baby used to one bottle a day. Finally, it also gives the father a wonderful opportunity to become more involved.

There are many types of bottles available, with each manufacturer claiming it provides the "best bottle" for your baby. Over the years I have tried and tested every available one, and the one that I have found to be the absolute best is the wide-necked design by "AVENT," available in baby specialty stores. The wide neck makes cleaning and filling easier, and I support their claim that the design of the nipple reduces the amount of air a baby gets into his stomach, being similar in shape to the mother's nipple. I suggest that you start off by using them with a slow-flow nipple. This will make your baby work as hard drinking the milk from the bottle as he does when he is breast-feeding.

For advice on the sterilizing equipment needed for your baby's feeding bottles, see page 20.

Equipment needed for bottle-feeding

Feeding bottles

For the reasons already discussed, I strongly advise mothers to pay a little extra money and purchase the wide-necked bottles described above. With babies who are taking all their milk from a bottle, it is important that the risk of developing colic or gas is kept to the minimum. I have learned from experience how babies being fed from cheaper bottles can develop gas. When called upon to help a baby with colic, I see an immediate improvement when I switch to feeding the baby with these wide-necked bottles. The designed nipple is flexible and allows the baby to suckle as he does at the breast; it lets air into the bottle and reduces the amount of air the baby takes in during a feed. By using these bottles, structuring the baby's feeds and following my routines, I have to date managed to solve all the colic problems with which I have been called upon to deal.

The wide-necked bottles also have the advantage that they can eventually be adapted to a feeding cup with soft spouts and handles. I would advise you to start off with five 8 oz bottles and three 4 oz bottles.

Nipples

Most feeding bottles come with a slow-flow nipple designed to meet the needs of newborns. All babies are different, and I find even from day one, some babies will feed better from a medium-flow nipple. By eight weeks I find that all my babies are feeding better from a medium-flow nipple. It is worthwhile stocking up with these extra nipples from the beginning.

Bottle brush

Proper and thorough cleaning of your baby's bottles is of the utmost importance. The best bottle brush comes with an extra-long plastic handle, which allows more force to be put into cleaning the bottles than with those that have either shorter plastic or wire handles.

Nipple brushes

Most mothers find it easier to clean the nipple by using their forefinger; however, if you have extra-long nails it may be worthwhile to invest in one of these brushes. The disadvantage with them is that it is all too easy to damage the hole of the nipple, resulting in the need to replace the nipples frequently. Of course, the same damage could be done with extra-long sharp nails!

Washing-up bowl

It is easier to organize and keep track of what is sterilized if all the dirty bottles are washed and sterilized at the same time. You will need somewhere to put the rinsed-out dirty bottles, etc., until they are ready to be sterilized. A large stainless steel or plastic bowl (ideally with a lid) can be used for this purpose; in addition, it can be used for washing the bottles and any other equipment that needs to be sterilized.

Sterilizer

Whether you are breast- or bottle-feeding, it is essential that all bottles and expressing equipment is sterilized properly. There are three main methods of sterilization: boiling all the equipment for ten minutes in a large pan, soaking in a sterilizing solution for two hours and rinsing with boiling water or using a specially designed electric steam sterilizer. I have tried and tested all three methods many times, and without doubt the easiest and fastest, and the one I believe to be the most efficient, is the steam sterilizer. It is well worth paying the extra money, for the convenience these sterilizers provide. A word of warning. Do not be tempted to purchase the microwave version of these sterilizers. This particular unit not only holds fewer bottles, but it also becomes a complete nuisance when you have to keep removing it to use the microwave for cooking.*

Electric bottle warmer

An electric bottle warmer is not really essential, as formula can always be heated by running the bottle under hot water. However, an electric bottle warmer can be very useful in the nursery for the 6:00 to 6:30 P.M. feed. There is a design that includes a bowl which fits on the top, and this can be used for keeping food warm, once your baby starts on solids.

Bottle insulator

This is a special type of thermos that is designed to keep bottles of boiled water warm. This can be very useful for traveling or for night feeds; it means that a feed can be prepared in seconds!

When buying one of these, it is advisable to purchase a small plastic three-section container; each section can hold the required scoops of milk powder for three different feeds. This avoids having to take the whole can of formula milk powder on a day out, or upstairs for the middle-of-the-night feed.

---

* Editor's Note: Here in the United States, parents usually take a more streamlined approach. Before using nipples, caps, rings or bottles for the first time, you should wash them then sterilize by submerging in boiling water for five minutes. Dry on a clean towel or rack. After the baby is three months old, you can clean equipment in hot, soapy water; however, you should sterilize bottles and nipples before each use. Consult your pediatrician for the latest information regarding sterilization and bottle feeding.

Clothes for the newborn

The range of baby clothes now available is enormous, and eager sales assistants will be more than happy to advise you on a very long list of so-called essentials for your newborn baby. While it can be fun choosing a wide array of garments for your baby, I urge parents to approach with caution. Newborn babies grow at an alarming rate and will outgrow most of the first-size clothes by the first month. Although it is important to have enough clothes to allow for the frequent changing of a newborn, it is foolish to end up having so many things hanging in the wardrobe that most of them never get worn. You will need to renew your baby's wardrobe at least three times in the first year, and even if you buy the cheapest of baby clothes it will still be a costly business.

I advise all parents to purchase only the basics until after the baby is born. When buying outfits for day wear, remember that you will probably receive many of these as presents, so only buy the minimum. As I mentioned earlier, you will have considerable opportunity during the first year for clothes shopping.

When choosing clothes for the first month, do not be tempted into buying brightly colored underwear or sleepwear. Believe me, it is impossible to keep these clean; newborn babies have a tendency to leak from both ends, and the stains, despite what soap powder manufacturers say, are impossible to remove in anything less than a scalding wash. Brightly colored garments soon lose their appearance if washed at a hot temperature, so leave the brighter colors for the outer garments.

Listed below are the basic items you will need for the first couple of months. I advise parents not to unwrap them until after the baby is born, so should you give birth to either a very large or very small baby they can be exchanged.

One-piece, snap-crotch T-shirts ("onesies")	6–8	Socks	2–3 pairs
Sleepers	4–6	Hats	2
Day outfits	4–6	Mittens	2 pairs
Sweaters	2–3	Receiving blankets	3
Snowsuit for a winter baby	1	Jacket	1

T-shirts

A newborn baby would normally wear a T-shirt both winter and summer except in very hot weather. The best fabric next to a baby's skin is 100 percent cotton, as polyester does not allow the baby's skin to breathe. If you want to avoid your beautiful new layette becoming grubby-looking or washed-out by the very hot wash needed to remove stains, stick to plain white, or white with a pale color pattern.

Without a doubt, the best style to buy is what is called a "onesie." It fastens under the baby's legs, has short sleeves and an envelope-type neckline, which enables you to either bring it over the baby's head easily, or to slip it on from the bottom. Avoid the traditional crossover type of T-shirts; they tend to ride up, leaving the chest bare, and the ties constantly come undone.

Sleepers

In recent years it has become fashionable to put babies to sleep in sleepers. While they may save a short amount of time on the laundry, they can cause hours of waking time in the night, as any experienced mother will tell you. You can spend 40 minutes feeding the baby and settling him, only to find he then fills his diaper. By the time you unpop all the fasteners, and struggle in the dim light to fasten them up again, even the most placid of babies is usually wide awake, possibly for another 40 minutes. As with T-shirts, 100 percent white cotton sleep sacks are best. The simpler the design, the better. Avoid anything with ties at the neck, and if there are ties at the bottom, remove them, as they could become undone and get caught around the baby's feet.

Day outfits

During the first couple of months many mothers find it easier to buy one-piece outfits, sometimes sold in packs of two or three. They should be made either of cotton or cotton and polyester. If possible, try to get 100 percent cotton. However, if something with 80 percent cotton and 20 percent man-made fiber takes your eye, buy it and use it for when the baby is out and about in his stroller or awake in his chair. Avoid putting him down to sleep all night in a garment that is not 100 percent cotton, as this could increase the risk of overheating.

Usually with these garments you can give them a quick wash by hand, as they are less likely to get stained. Obviously it allows you a greater choice of colors, when you do not have to worry about stains.

When choosing a garment, always try to find one that opens up either across the back or inside the legs, as it saves you having to undress the baby totally every time he needs a diaper change. Try to buy at least a couple of overalls without feet and with matching T-shirts. They last a bit longer than an all-in-one, and the tops can be interchanged if the baby spits up a lot. Choose ones in a soft velour-type fabric for very young babies.

Sweaters

If you have a summer baby, you could probably get away with just two sweaters, ideally in cotton. With a winter baby it is best to have at least three. Although it is often hard to find, I firmly believe that wool is best for the winter. As long as the baby has a cotton garment next to his skin, there should be no cause for irritation and the simpler the design the better. While the very lacy-patterned garments with ribbons are enchanting, be aware that little fingers can get entangled in these if they become undone, which could be dangerous. Perhaps two plain ones, and one fancier one for special occasions would be the answer.

Socks

Old-fashioned bootees and socks with fancy ribbons should be avoided, and should only be used for special occasions as they are dangerous for the same reasons: entangling little fingers and toes. Therefore simple socks, again in cotton or wool, are by far the most practical. It is probably worth mentioning here that no matter how cute they seem, shoes are not a good idea for small babies, as they could harm their soft bones.

Hats

In the summer it is important that you buy a cotton hat with a brim to protect your baby's head and face from the sun. Ideally the brim should go right around the back of the neck. In the spring and autumn, it is possible to buy knitted cotton hats, which are more than adequate on cooler days. During the winter on very cold days, I would advise that a very fine wool bonnet is preferable. If the baby has very sensitive skin, put a very thin cotton hat underneath it.

Mittens

I believe that small babies do not like their hands being covered up, as they use them to touch, feel and explore everything with which they come in close contact. However, if your baby has very sharp nails, you could try the plain fine cotton mitts made for this purpose. In very cold weather use simple wool mittens; again, put cotton ones underneath if your baby has sensitive skin.

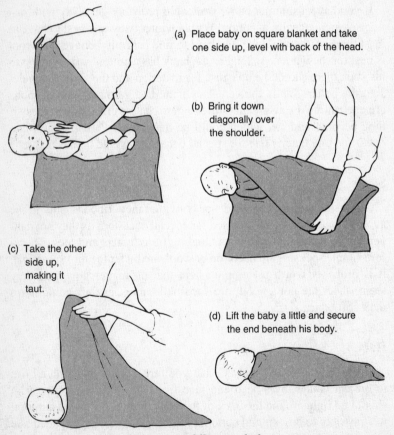

(a) Place baby on square blanket and take one side up, level with back of the head.

(b) Bring it down diagonally over the shoulder.

(c) Take the other side up, making it taut.

(d) Lift the baby a little and secure the end beneath his body.

How to swaddle your baby

Blanket

I firmly believe that during the first few weeks all babies sleep better when swaddled. Whether you choose a blanket or a shawl to swaddle your baby it should always be made of a very lightweight 100 percent cotton fabric that has a slight stretch to it. When swaddling the baby, it is important not to double the blanket. To avoid overheating, always swaddle the baby in a single layer. Remember when putting your baby to sleep swaddled to reduce the number of blankets in the crib.

Snowsuit

When choosing a snowsuit for a winter baby, always buy it at least two sizes too big, as this allows plenty of room for growth. Avoid fancy designs with fur around the hood or dangling laces, and choose one in an easy-care washable fabric. For very small babies one with snaps is preferable to one with a zipper, which often digs into the baby's chin.

Jacket

A lightweight jacket can be useful for babies born at any time of the year. In the summer it can be worn on chilly days, and in the winter it can be worn on milder days. As with the snowsuit, choose a simple design in a washable fabric, preferably with buttons, and again, two sizes too big.

Your baby's laundry

Having spent a considerable amount of time and money on your baby's wardrobe, it is well worth the effort to be very fussy about caring for it. Because young babies grow out of their clothes so quickly, it should be possible to pass them on to any brother or sister that follows. Sadly this often cannot be achieved, as poor laundering means that a whole new layette is needed for the next baby.

The following guidelines will help keep your baby's laundry in tip-top condition.

• Laundry should be sorted into different colored lots.
• Bedding, sheets and bibs need to be washed in very hot water to

get rid of bacteria caused by milk stains and to eliminate the house dust mite, which can trigger off allergies in very young babies.

- Load the washing machine no more than two-thirds full so that the clothes are rinsed thoroughly.
- Stains should always be treated before washing.

Whites: hot

Anything that is stained should be soaked overnight in a prewash solution, then washed in hot water. Everything should be 100 percent cotton, and bibs or towels with a colored trim should have been tested for color run by washing separately for the first few washes. Sheets, T-shirts, bibs, socks and white sleep suits and nighties can also go in hot water if they are not very dirty. If they have not been soaked and are very dirty, they should be treated with a prewash and laundered in hot water. Towels and facecloths should be washed and dried together, separate from other clothes. Remember, always use detergents made especially for baby clothes. They have fewer additives that can irritate baby's sensitive skin.

Light colors: warm

Most day clothes need only a very quick wash in the delicate cycle. Anything stained should be soaked first overnight in cold water and a prewash and rinsed before washing.

Dark colors: cold

Any dark outfits must be washed separately from the light colors even if they do not run; to mix the two will only result in the lighter colors taking on a gray tinge. Anything stained should be soaked first overnight in cold water and prewash solution.

Delicates: hand wash

Even if the label says "machine wash," it is better to hand wash using a very small amount of gentle soap mixed with lukewarm water. Always squeeze the garment gently in the water when washing and rinsing; never wring, twist or allow a delicate garment to hang down. Rinse thoroughly in cool running water, gently squeeze out excess water, then roll in a clean, dry white towel for a few hours. Finally, gently pull into shape and either dry flat or hang across a drying screen. Never hang up sweaters from the bottom.

Corduroy and dark clothes

To avoid fading and shadowing, dry these on the cool cycle for no more than 15 minutes. Then pull the clothes into shape and hang them up on hangers to dry. In this way they may not need to be ironed.

❀ 2 ❀

After the birth

Leaving the hospital

During your stay in the hospital, you may be like many of my mothers, counting the hours until you leave. However, when the actual day arrives, do not be surprised if you have feelings of fear and anxiety. This is very normal, especially for first-time mothers who are faced with the sudden realization that they are totally responsible for all the needs of this very precious tiny human being. Without the help and support of the nursing staff, everything can suddenly seem very overwhelming.

To eliminate these feelings as soon as possible, it is very important that you plan your homecoming very carefully. It is essential that all family and friends are warned well in advance that you wish to keep the first week as calm and quiet as possible.

Obviously a new baby always brings much joy and excitement, and you do not want to deny family and close friends the pleasure of sharing this. However, it is critical that your baby has time to adjust to his new surroundings. Some babies can be a little unsettled on leaving the hospital, and this can often be made much worse when they are subjected to endless handling, passed from one person to another. It is also essential that you allow time for you and your husband to get used to having this very special little person in your life, and even more importantly, time to learn how to meet his many very different needs.

This is very difficult to achieve if you have a constant stream of visitors during the first week, and the phone never stops ringing.

The calmer and quieter things are, the sooner you will start to feel confident about caring for your baby. Do not feel guilty about delaying visits from friends for the first week or so. The prime consideration must be your baby, especially in the early days of breast-feeding, as tiredness can seriously affect your milk production. Babies are also sensitive to their mother's emotions, and your baby will become very unsettled if he senses you are overtired and stressed.

If your husband is not able to take time off work for you and the baby's first week at home, try to arrange some sort of help. If your mother (or mother-in-law) will help, but not try to take over, and if she respects that you want to do things your own way, then see if she can come for a few days. If she lives near enough to stop by for a few hours each day, do not be afraid to request help with the cooking of meals, shopping or laundry. The more rest you can get in the first week at home, the better.

Breast-feeding: what to expect

Babies often become unsettled for the first few days at home. A well-meaning grandmother may try to convince you that your baby's fretfulness is due to hunger, that you are probably not producing enough milk to satisfy him or that your milk is of poor quality. These remarks, no matter how well-intentioned they are, can be very distressing for a new mother, who desperately wants breast-feeding to be a success. Please be reassured that once your milk is in, if your baby totally empties a breast at every feed and is offered the other one, he will not go hungry. In my experience, formula-fed babies can be just as fretful the first few days at home, which discounts the "hunger myth."

Remember that your baby needs to feed little and often during the first week to help stimulate a good milk supply. Unless advised by the hospital, ignore any pressure to give him a little formula. This is old-fashioned advice and the fastest way to end up formula feeding. The exceptions to this rule would be if you had suffered a very bad delivery and were left feeling very weak, or if you had given birth to a very large baby. In these circumstances I would suggest that the baby was given one formula feed late at night, to allow the mother some much-needed rest.

If you follow my guidelines for establishing breast-feeding in Chapter 4 (see page 55), along with my other routines, you will find that you will very quickly build up a good milk supply and have a very contented and well-fed baby. I have mothers who, by following my advice, manage successfully to breast-feed their second, third and fourth babies.

During the first few weeks

During the first few weeks, aim to wake your baby up at 7:00 A.M. every morning, regardless of how long he has slept in the night. It is the quickest way to establish a regular feeding pattern. Follow the feeding times on the schedule. It will ensure that your baby gets enough food during the day, which should mean only one waking in the night. If during the first month your baby suddenly sleeps through to 4:00 or 5:00 A.M., do not be tempted to let him sleep past 7:00 A.M. Wake him up as usual and give him a short feed to keep him on track for the rest of the day. Refer to the feeding charts in Chapter 4 (pages 73 and 79), to see how quickly things can go wrong if your baby sleeps past 7:00 A.M.

In the first few weeks if you express and freeze any extra milk you have in the early part of the day, you will ensure that when your baby goes through a growth spurt at three weeks, you will easily be able to meet his increased demands. It could also be used to top up your baby after the 6:15 P.M. feed if he is not settling and you feel the reason could be your milk is low. During growth spurts if you decrease your expressing by 1 oz at the early morning feeds, your baby will automatically receive the extra milk he needs. This avoids the need to go back to three hourly feedings to increase your milk supply, which would more than likely be the case if you did not express in the first few weeks.

Bottle-feeding: what to expect

Within a few days most formula-fed babies have established some sort of feeding pattern, if they are drinking the required amount of formula at each feed for their weight. Do not be tempted to let your baby go longer than four hours between feeds during the day. To ensure that he only wakes for one feeding in the night, he needs to take the majority of his daily milk requirements between 7:00 A.M. and 11:00 P.M. A baby who is allowed to sleep five to six hours between feeds during the day would actually be two feeds short by 11:00 P.M. He would more than likely wake up two or three times in the night to try and satisfy his hunger. When this happens a mother is often so tired that she allows him to sleep well past the 7:00 A.M. feed in the morning, and a pattern emerges of the baby feeding more in the night than during the day.

Regardless of when your baby feeds in the night, do not be tempted to let him sleep past 7:00 A.M. If he has fed at 5:00 or 6:00 A.M., he will not be really hungry at 7:00 A.M., but offer him a 30–60 ml (1–2 oz) feed around 7:30 A.M. This will ensure that he gets through happily to the 10:00 to 10:30 A.M. feed. If he has slept to 5:00 A.M. or 6:00 A.M. and you do not give him a small feeding, he will get hungry nearer 9:00 A.M. and not settle for his nap. This will spoil the routine of altering the times for all his naps and feeds. Regardless of whether they are breast- or bottle-fed, the only way to keep babies in a good routine is to begin the day at 7:00 A.M.

Occasionally there are babies who will drink a full feed in 10–15 minutes and look for more. These babies are often referred to as "hungrier babies"; the reality is that these babies are usually "sucky" babies, not hungrier ones. Because they have such a strong suck, they are able to finish the bottle very quickly. Sucking is not only a means of feeding for a baby, but in the early days one of their natural pleasures. If your baby is taking the required amount of formula at each feed very quickly, and looking for more, it may be worthwhile trying a nipple with a smaller hole. Offering him a pacifier after he feeds may also help satisfy his "sucking needs." However, if your baby takes longer than 20 minutes to drink the first couple of ounces, it could be that the hole on the nipple is too small and it would be advisable to try the next size.

It is very easy for bottle-fed babies to gain weight too quickly if they are allowed to have feeds well in excess of the amounts recommended for their weight. While a few ounces a day extra should not create a problem, a baby who is overeating and regularly putting on more than 8 oz each week will eventually become too fat and reach a stage where milk alone is not enough to satisfy his hunger. If this happens before the recommended age for giving solids, it can create a real problem.

The first few weeks

During the first few weeks, try to stick to the daily recommended amounts for your baby's weight, give or take a few ounces. If your baby seems very "sucky," consider giving him a pacifier. As long as it is used with discretion, and he is not allowed to fall asleep with it in his mouth or in the crib, a problem should not arise. Bottle-fed babies can become quite distracted when feeding, as they have more opportunity to look around, so try to keep feeding time calm and quiet. Do not over-stimulate or talk to him too much, as this can cause him to lose interest in the feed. Be guided by your baby as to when he is ready to be burped. If the air does not come up within a few minutes, leave it and try later. Keep referring to the sections on establishing bottle feeding and structuring milk feeds in Chapter 4, to make sure you increase the right feeds at the correct times.

Sleepy feeder

Sometimes a very sleepy baby may be inclined to keep dozing during the feed, but if he does not take the required amount, he will end up wanting to feed again in an hour or two. This is a good time to change his diaper and burp him and encourage him to finish his feed. Making a little effort in the early days to keep your baby awake enough to drink the correct amount at each feed, and at the times given on the routine, will in the long term be well worthwhile. Some babies will take half the feed, have a stretch and kick for 10–15 minutes and then be happy to take the rest. During the first month allow up to 45 minutes for a feed.

Common problems

Burping

It is important to follow your baby's lead regarding when to stop and burp him. If you constantly interrupt his feed to try and get a burp, he will be more likely to get so upset and frustrated that the crying will cause more gas than the feed itself. Time and time again I watch babies being thumped endlessly on the back, the mother refusing to continue with the feed as she is convinced the baby has gas. The reality is that very few babies need to be burped more than once during a feed and once at the end.

A breast-feeding baby will pull himself off the breast when he is ready to burp. If he has not done so by the end of the first breast, you can try burping before putting him on the second breast. Bottle-fed babies will normally drink half to three quarters of their feed and pull themselves off to be burped. Regardless of whether you are breast-feeding or bottle-feeding, if you adopt the correct holding position, as illustrated below, your baby should bring his gas up quickly and easily both during and at the end of the feed. If your baby does not burp within a few minutes, it is best to leave it and try later. More often than not he will burp after he has been laid flat for his diaper change.

Occasionally a baby passing excessive gas from his rear end can suffer considerable discomfort and become very distressed. A breast-

The correct burping position

feeding mother should keep a close eye on her diet to see if a particular food or drink is causing the gas. Citrus fruits or drinks taken in excess can sometimes cause severe gas in some babies. The other culprits are chocolate and excessive dairy intake.

Special care should be taken to make sure that the baby is reaching the hind milk. Too much fore milk can cause explosive bowel movements and excessive gas.

With a bottle-fed baby who is already feeding from the special anticolic bottles, the cause of the excessive gas is usually overfeeding. If your baby is regularly drinking 3–6 oz a day more than the amount advised on the packet, and constantly putting on in excess of 8 oz of weight each week, cut back on a couple of his feeds (either the 2:30 P.M. or the 5:00 P.M.) for a few days to see if there is any improvement. A "sucky" baby could be offered a pacifier after the smaller feeds to satisfy his sucking needs.

Sometimes a nipple with a hole either too small or too large for your baby's needs could cause excessive gas. Experiment with the different sizes of nipples; sometimes using a smaller hole at a couple of the feeds can help a baby who is drinking some of his feeds too quickly.

Spitting up

It is very common for some babies to bring up a small amount of milk while being burped or after a feed. It is called spitting up, and for most babies it does not create a problem. However, if your baby is regularly gaining more than 8 oz of weight each week, it could be that he is drinking too much. With a bottle-fed baby the problem is easily solved as you are able to see how much the baby is drinking and therefore slightly reduce the amount at the feeds during which he appears to spit up more. It is more difficult to tell how much a breast-fed baby is drinking. But by keeping a note of which feeds cause more spitting up, and reducing the time on the breast at those feeds, the spitting up may be reduced.

If your baby is spitting up excessively and not gaining weight, it could be that he is suffering from a condition called "reflux." If your baby does have reflux, your doctor can prescribe a medication to be given either before or with a feed, which helps keep the milk down. With babies who are inclined to bring up milk, it is important to keep them as upright as possible after a feed, and special care should be taken when burping.

**Any baby bringing up an entire feed twice in a row should be
seen by a doctor immediately.**

Hiccups

Hiccups are very normal among tiny babies, and very few get distressed by them. Hiccups often happen after a feed. If it has been a
nighttime feed and your baby is due to go down for a sleep, it is advisable to go ahead and put him down regardless. If you wait until the hiccups have finished, there is a bigger chance of him falling asleep in
your arms, which is something to be avoided at all costs.

Colic

Colic is a common problem for babies under three months. It can
make life miserable for the baby and the parents, and to date there is no
cure for it. There are over-the-counter medications, but most parents
with a baby suffering from severe colic say they are of little help. Although a baby can suffer from colic at any time of the day, the most
common time seems to be between 6:00 P.M. and midnight. Parents resort to endless feeding, rocking, patting, driving the baby around the
block, most of which seem to bring little or no relief. Colic usually dis-
appears by four months of age, but by that time the baby has usually
learned all the wrong sleep associations, so the parents are no further
ahead.

Parents who contact me for help with their "colicky baby" describe
how the baby screams, often for hours at a time, thrashes madly and
keeps bringing up his legs in pain. These babies all seem to have one
thing in common: they are all being fed on demand. Feeding this way
all too often leads to the baby having another feed before the first one
has been digested, one of the things that I believe may cause colic. (See
also the advice on feeding bottles on pages 17–18.)

Not one of the babies I have cared for has ever suffered from colic,
and I am convinced that it is because I structure their feeding and sleeping from day one. When I do go in to help an older baby who is suffering from colic, it seems to disappear within 24 hours of him being
put on to the routine. With babies that are feeding two or three times a
night, depending on their age and weight I either cut out the feeds altogether or reduce them to one a night. When the baby wakes in the night,
I would give 4 oz of cool boiled water mixed with half a teaspoon of

sugar to settle him. At this stage I find plain boiled water does not have the same effect. The following day I would wake the baby at 7:00 A.M., regardless of how little sleep he had had in the night, and then proceed with the routine throughout the day to 6:30 P.M. At this time I would always offer a breast-fed baby a small amount of expressed milk to ensure that he has had enough to drink. This avoids him needing to feed again in two hours, which is a common pattern of babies suffering from colic. With a bottle-fed baby, I always make sure that the 2:30 P.M. feed is smaller so that he feeds well at 6:30 P.M.

Often I find that bottle-fed babies suffering from colic are being given very large feeds at 3:00 P.M. or 4:00 P.M. in the day, resulting in a poor feed at 6:30 P.M. Like the breast-fed baby, they would then need to feed again in a couple of hours.

More often than not the baby settles well the first night, but occasionally I may get a baby who has developed the wrong sleep associations as a result of the colic. With these babies I use the controlled crying method of sleep training, and within three to four nights they are going down happily and sleeping well until the 10:30 P.M. feed. Because they have slept well and have gone a full four hours since their last feed, they feed well and will go on to last for an even longer spell in the night. Depending on their age, they are given either a feed or sugar water. A baby of three months or older who is capable of going from the last feed through to 6:00 A.M. or 7:00 A.M. should be given sugar water for a week. Once the pattern of one night waking is established, gradually reduce the amount of sugar until he is taking plain water.

This method, along with the routines, will encourage a baby who has suffered from colic and developed the wrong sleep associations to sleep through the night, normally within a couple of weeks. I cannot stress strongly enough that the success of this method very much depends on the use of the sugar water during the first week. Plain water does not have the same success. I am not sure why the sugar water method works. It is a tip I picked up from an older maternity nurse over 25 years ago, and it has never failed me. Parents are often concerned that it will encourage their babies to develop a sweet tooth, or even worse rot their teeth. Because of the short period of time the sugar water is used, I have never seen any of these problems evolve. I am also pleased to say that my advice has now been backed up by recent research on colic by Dr. Peter Lewindon of the Royal Children's Hospital, Brisbane, Australia. Research shows that sugar stimulates the body's natural painkillers and that some babies suffering from colic can be helped by the sugar-water solution.

Reflux

Sometimes a baby displaying all the symptoms of colic actually has a condition called gastro-esophageal reflux. Because the muscle at the lower end of the esophagus is too weak to keep the milk in the baby's stomach, it comes back up, along with acid from the stomach, causing a very painful burning sensation in the esophagus. Excessive spitting up is one of the symptoms of reflux. However, not all babies with reflux actually spit up the milk, and these babies can often be misdiagnosed as having colic. They are often very difficult to feed, constantly arching their backs and screaming during a feed. They also tend to get very irritable when laid flat and no amount of cuddling or rocking will calm them when they are like this. If your baby displays these symptoms, insist that your doctor does a reflux test. I have seen too many cases of babies being diagnosed as having colic, when in fact they were suffering from reflux, despite not being sick. It is important that a baby with reflux is not overfed and is kept as upright as possible during and after feeding. Some babies may need medication for several months until the muscles tighten up. Fortunately the majority of babies outgrow the condition by the time they reach one year old.

Alice: aged six weeks

Alice was four weeks old when I went to help care for her. I had helped look after her elder brother Patrick, then aged two, for six weeks when he was born. He had been a model baby and had gone into the routine from day one. He slept through the night at six weeks and had continued to do so ever since; he had always been a good feeder and a very easy baby. I felt confident that the mother would only need me for four weeks with the second baby, as she had always shown an excellent understanding of sleep rhythms, the importance of the right sleep associations and the correct structuring of feeds.

It therefore came as a bit of a shock to find that Alice was not quite in "the routine." Her sleeping pattern was fine: she settled well at 7:00 P.M., I woke her at 10:00 P.M., she fed well and would sleep until 5:00 A.M. and her lunchtime sleep was also good. The problem was that she would not be put down to sleep during the day. I was rather surprised to find her mother carrying her everywhere, as she had been insistent when Patrick was a baby that he should learn to sit happily in his chair or go on his play mat for short spells. After several days of helping care for Alice, I could see why she had to be held the whole time, as the minute she was put on the floor or in her bouncy chair, she went berserk. In the long term, when the mother was going to have to care for both children, we could see that this was going to be a problem. Alice's six-week check with the doctor only confirmed what we already knew, that for her age she was very advanced, both mentally and physically. However, he could offer no real advice on how to make life happier for her and for the rest of us during the day.

In desperation we were referred to a pediatrician. I suggested that although Alice never brought up any milk, she did show some behavior signs of "reflux." He was adamant that she did not have reflux and suggested that perhaps we were spoiling her and that we should be stricter about leaving her in her chair. Over the two weeks that followed, despite very small last feeds at 7:00 P.M. and 10:00 P.M., Alice would sleep well at night. However, the days got worse, and she screamed and screamed and screamed. Things came to a head when she started to scream and arch her back the minute we tried to feed her. We went to see the pediatrician for the second time, as I was convinced she did have reflux, but he was just as adamant as the previous time, and because she was never sick said it could not be reflux. Two more weeks passed with Alice's behavior getting worse and worse. A third visit was booked to the pediatrician. This time the mother was insistent that the test be done and agreed to pay for it herself. The result came back positive: Alice had very serious reflux. She was given medication, and her behavior immediately began to improve; she would spend time on her play mat happily looking at her toys and the feedings got easier.

The sad thing about Alice is that as a very small baby she must have suffered a lot of pain. All too often babies are dismissed as being difficult or having colic, when in fact they are suffering from reflux, which is a problem that a great many doctors seem keen not to acknowledge.

Pacifiers

The majority of baby care experts frown upon the use of a pacifier, claiming that a sucky baby should be allowed to find his thumb. While the majority of very young babies are able to find their thumb, I have yet to see one who can keep it in his mouth long enough to achieve any sucking pleasure. In reality, it takes nearly three months for a baby to develop enough coordination to keep his thumb in his mouth for any length of time.

I am amazed how some parents prefer to stick their own fingers in their baby's mouth and spend hour after hour rocking and walking the floor with their baby rather than give him a pacifier. They choose to end up with a very demanding baby who refuses to be put down or even to sit for 15 minutes in a baby chair, just because they do not want to give him a pacifier.

If used with discretion I think a pacifier can be a great asset, especially for a sucky baby. However, I must stress the importance of never allowing your baby to have the pacifier in his crib or allowing him to suck himself to sleep on the pacifier. By all means use it to calm him and if necessary to settle him at sleep times, **but remove it before he falls asleep.** He may yell for a short time, but he will soon learn not to expect it while sleeping. Allowing a baby to fall asleep with a pacifier in his mouth is one of the worst sleep association problems to try and solve. He can end up waking several times a night, and each time he will expect the pacifier to get back to sleep. This problem can easily be avoided if the pacifier is removed just before he drops off to sleep.

I have used pacifiers with a great number of my babies and have not encountered any serious problems. By being selective in their use, I find that by the age of three months the majority of my babies are rejecting them. If a baby reaches four months and is still using the pacifier, I would gradually wean him from using it over a period of two weeks; any longer could lead to real attachment problems.

There are two types of pacifiers available. One has a round cherry-type nipple; the other has a flat-shaped nipple, which is called an orthodontic nipple. Some experts claim that the orthodontic pacifier shape is better for the baby's mouth, but the problem with this type is that most young babies cannot hold them in for very long. I tend to use the cherry-type nipple, and so far none of my babies appears to have developed an open bite, which is often the result of a pacifier being used excessively once the teeth have come through. Whichever type of pacifier you choose, buy several, thus allowing them to be changed frequently. The utmost attention should be paid to cleanliness when using a pacifier; it should be washed and sterilized after each use. Never clean it by licking it, as one sees so many parents do; there are more germs and bacteria in the mouth than you could believe.*

Crying

I have read in many leading baby books that most young babies cry on average a total of two hours in a day. This is also the information given by the Thomas Coram Research Unit at London University. They also claim that at six weeks crying reaches a peak, with 25 percent of babies crying and fussing for at least four hours a day. Dr. St. James-Roberts also claims that 40 percent of the crying occurs between 6:00 P.M. and midnight. Dutch researchers Van de Rijt and Plooij, authors of *Why They Cry* (Thorsons), have spent over 20 years studying baby development, and they claim that babies become troublesome and demanding when they are going through one of the seven major neurological changes that occur during the first year.

With very young babies I have noticed that they do go through a more unsettled stage around three weeks and six weeks, which tends to coincide with growth spurts. However, I would be absolutely horrified if any of my babies cried for even one hour a day, let alone two to four hours! The one thing that parents comment upon time and time again is how happy their baby is on the routine. Of course my babies do cry; some may cry when they have their diaper changed, others cry when having their faces washed and a few try to fight sleep when put in their cribs. With the ones that fight sleep, because I know they are well fed, burped and ready to sleep, I am very strict. I would let them fuss and yell for 10–20 minutes until they have settled themselves. This is the only real crying I experience, and even then it is with the minority of my babies and lasts for no longer than a week or two. Understandably all parents hate to hear their baby cry; many are worried that to put their baby down in a crib to sleep and leave him to cry like this could be psychologically damaging. I would like to reassure you that provided your baby has been well fed, and that you have followed the routines regarding awake periods and wind-down time, your baby will not suf-

---

* Editor's Note: It's perfectly acceptable to follow these guidelines instead. Before the first use, wash and then sterilize your baby's pacifier in boiling water for five minutes. (Let it cool before giving it to your child.) After that, clean in soapy water or run it through a cycle on the top rack of your dishwasher.

fer psychological damage. In the long term you will have a happy, contented baby who has learned to settle himself to sleep. Many parents who have followed the demand method with the first baby, and my routines with their second baby, would confirm wholeheartedly that my methods are by far the best and, in the long term, the easiest.

Marc Weissbluth M.D., Director of the Sleep Disorders Center at the Children's Memorial Hospital, Chicago, says in his book *Healthy Sleep Habits, Happy Child* (Ballantine/Random House) that parents should remember they are allowing their baby to cry, not making him cry. He also says that it will be much harder for an older baby to learn how to settle himself. Therefore, do not feel guilty or cruel if you have to allow a short spell of crying when your baby is going off to sleep. He will very quickly learn to settle himself, as long as you have made sure he is well fed, and has been awake enough, but not so long that he is overtired.

Overtiredness and not allowing the baby to settle himself to sleep are, I believe, the major reasons for excessive crying. No baby under four months should be allowed to stay awake for longer than two hours at a stretch. Care should also be taken not to overstimulate the baby 30 minutes prior to being put to bed. Time and time again these points are proved to be true, when I do my sleep consultations. Parents are amazed that with careful structuring of sleep and feeding their baby's crying time is reduced significantly within days. Unless your baby has a medical condition, I would be very surprised if you experienced much crying from him, provided of course you are following the routines to the letter. (See also page 84.)

Bonding: what to expect

The amount of attention and focus currently given by the media to "a mother's love" and "bonding" gives the impression that the majority of mothers do not know how to love their babies. Hardly a day passes without a magazine or newspaper featuring a double-page spread of some celebrity mother, looking absolutely radiant as she cradles her designer-clad newborn baby. The birth, regardless of how long or difficult it was, she describes as the most wonderful, joyful and enriching experience of her life.

Within weeks, in a follow-up article, she claims that for the first time in her life she feels emotionally fulfilled and blissfully happy. Despite her short experience of motherhood, she feels qualified enough to give advice on the importance of love and bonding; she claims that feeding on demand and having a baby share the marital bed is the only way of true bonding. She and the baby now have a wonderful, often "spiritual" relationship and understand each other totally. In this short time she also has managed (presumably between two hourly breast-feeds) to fit in a leading part in the next Oscar Award–winning film, write a best-selling novel or stage a return to the catwalk, showing the world how easy it is to get back into shape after giving birth.

All this, she claims, is achieved without hired help as she wants the baby to grow up in a normal environment. Yet we never see such a mother struggling to board the number 52 bus, with a bag of Pampers in one hand, several bags of shopping in the other and the baby hanging in a sling. It is not surprising, with all the pressure created by the media and these "perfect mothers," that many "normal mothers" feel very inadequate during the first few weeks. The reality is that for the majority of mothers without paid help, along with the feelings of joy and love, there can be those of sheer exhaustion from nights of broken sleep and feelings of failure and frustration when an irritable baby cannot be calmed. These feelings can lead a mother to believe that she does not love her baby enough or is not bonding properly.

True bonding is something that evolves over many weeks and months. Do not be pressured into believing that "demand feeding and sleeping" is the only way to bond with your baby. Time and time again I get calls from depressed mothers who are feeling so guilty and resentful that they are not bonding with their babies. The real problem stems not from the lack of bonding but from the lack of sleep. The truth is that for any normal mother, weeks of sleep deprivation, caused by endless middle-of-the-night feedings, is bound to hamper bonding.

Within a short time of getting the baby on my routine, I find the mother's depression and resentfulness disappear. It is much easier to bond with a happy, contented baby than an irritable, fretful one who needs constant feeding and rocking. My routines will help you understand what your baby's needs really are and to know how to fulfill those needs, making the bonding process a happy and more enjoyable one.

❀ 3 ❀

Understanding your baby's sleep

S leep is probably the most misunderstood and confusing aspect of parenthood. The misconception is that for the first few weeks, all the baby will do is feed and sleep. While many do, the fact that there are sleep clinics in the United States specially for babies and children is proof that a great many do not.* If your newborn or young baby is one of the latter, tense, fretful and difficult to settle, please take heart as this need not be a reflection of your baby's future sleep habits.

Accomplishing a regular sleep pattern can be achieved without distress to you or your baby by observing the guidelines I have laid out in this book for your baby's routine. By being patient, consistent and allowing time for my routine to be established, you can avoid the agony of months of sleepless nights that so many parents go through. It has worked for hundreds of my babies and their parents, so it can work for you!

The golden rule, if you want your baby to sleep through the night from an early age and ensure a long-term healthy sleep pattern, is to establish the right associations and structure your baby's feeds from the day you arrive home from the hospital. The advice given in most of the baby books and by hospital staff is that newborn babies should feed on

---

* Editor's Note: You can obtain a current listing of sleep centers from: American Sleep Disorders Association, 1610 Fourteenth Street NW, Suite 300, Rochester, MN 55901, or use their Web site: www.asda.org.

demand as often and for as long as they need. You will be told to accept that your baby's erratic sleeping and feeding patterns are normal and that things will improve by three months of age. I receive endless phone calls and letters from distraught mothers whose infants, aged anywhere between three months and three years, have serious sleep and feeding problems, which continually disproves the theory that babies will put themselves into a routine by three months. Even if a baby does do this, it is unlikely to be a routine that fits in with the rest of the family.

While some experts would agree that some babies are capable of sleeping through the night by three months, they do not stress the importance of guiding the baby toward this goal. The innocent and weary mother believes in a miraculous improvement at three months, but this is unlikely to happen if her baby has not learned the difference between day and night, naps and the long sleep, and if the parent has not learned how to structure feeds which need to be established from day one.

Demand feeding

The phrase "demand feeding" is used time and time again, misleading a new mother into believing that any sort of routine in the early days could deny her baby nutritionally and, according to some experts, emotionally. While I would agree totally that the old-fashioned four hourly routine of feeding, whether breast or bottle, is not natural to newborn babies, I feel the term "feeding on demand" is used too loosely. All too often I get desperate telephone calls from the maternity wards. The cry for help is nearly always the same. The baby is feeding up to an hour at a time, every two hours from 6:00 P.M. until 5:00 A.M. The mother is usually exhausted and starting to suffer from cracked nipples.

When I ask what the baby is like during the day, the usual reply is: "He's so good during the day, he will feed then go four hours or longer." The experts are forever telling us that a newborn baby can need as many as 8 to 12 feeds a day. It is not surprising then that a baby who has only four or even fewer feeds between 6:00 A.M. and 6:00 P.M. is going to wake up many times in the night to satisfy his daily needs. Despite the advice that newborns need so many feeds in the day, it never ceases to amaze me that hospital staff actually encourage new mothers to let their babies sleep for long spells in the day to prepare them for the tough night ahead. The pattern for sleepless nights unfortunately is often set before mother and baby leave the hospital.

Once home, new parents become totally exhausted as they start to experience more and more difficulty in settling the baby. In desperation they follow the advice given in nearly all the current baby books available: rock the baby to sleep, feed the baby to sleep, drive the baby around in the car until he falls asleep and, if all else fails, take the baby into bed.

It is generally accepted by most of the baby experts that the behavior of the baby is normal and this way of dealing with the problem is normal. After months of sleepless nights and exhausting days with the baby still feeding every two or three hours, many parents ask their pediatrician to refer them to a baby sleep clinic. Or they purchase one or several of the many books on how to get your baby to sleep through the night, only to be told they got it all wrong in the first place. The real reason their baby is unable to sleep well is because he has the wrong associations with going to sleep: feeding, rocking, patting, etc.

Dilly Dawes, a leading child psychotherapist with the Tavistock clinic, and David Messer at the University of Herefordshire have both done extensive research into the sleeping patterns of babies and young children. Both come to the same conclusion, that a baby's sleeping habits can be determined by the prenatal expectations of the mother. Dilly describes mothers as either "regulators" or "facilitators." The regulator mother has very clear ideas about how the baby should fit into her life. The facilitator mother tries to adapt to suit her baby's inclinations. Dilly claims that regulators are less likely to have problems than facilitators. David Messer seems to back this up. He claims that if a mother expects to get up several times a night, she probably will.

My own experience finds this behavior to be true of many parents. But the facilitator mother's attitude will often change once she fully understands that her baby is unable to sleep well because of the wrong associations he has learned from her in order to get to sleep. In order to get these associations correct, it is important that you establish whether your baby is really ready to sleep. An understanding of the natural sleep rhythms of very young babies is essential, otherwise you will be fighting a losing battle.

Sleep rhythms

Most of the leading experts agree that a newborn baby will sleep approximately 16 hours a day in the first few weeks. This sleep is broken up into a series of short and longer sleeps. In the early days sleep is very much linked to the baby's need to feed little and often. It can take well up to an hour to feed, burp and change the baby, after which time he falls quickly into a deep sleep, often sleeping through to the next feed. It is easy to see why new parents get lulled into a false sense of security. The baby does exactly what the textbooks say. Over a 24-hour period, with six to eight feeds a day lasting between 45 minutes and one hour, the baby ends up sleeping approximately 16 hours a day.

Usually between the third and fourth week, the baby becomes more alert, and will not fall straight into a deep sleep after feeding. The anxious parents, believing that the baby should fall asleep straight after feeding, start to resort to some or all of the methods mentioned earlier. They do not realize that the behavior of the baby is totally normal.

It is around this age that the different stages of sleep become more apparent. Like adults, babies go through different stages of sleep. They drift from light sleep into a dreamlike sleep known as REM sleep, then into a deep sleep. The cycle is much shorter than that of an adult, lasting approximately 45 minutes to one hour. While some babies only stir when they drift into light sleep, others will wake up fully. If the baby is due for a feed, this does not create a problem. However, if it is only one hour since the baby fed, and the baby does not learn to settle himself, a real problem can develop over the months ahead.

Recent research has shown that all babies drift into light sleep and wake up approximately the same number of times during the night. Only the poor sleepers are unable to drift back into deep sleep, because they are used to being helped to sleep by one or all of the methods mentioned earlier.

If you want your baby to develop good sleep habits from an early age, it is important to avoid the wrong sleep associations. My routines are structured so that your baby feeds well, never gets overtired, and does not learn the wrong associations when going to sleep.

Your questions answered

Q **How many hours sleep a day does my newborn baby need?**

A • Depending on weight and whether the baby was premature, most babies need approximately 16 hours a day, broken up into a series of short and long sleeps.

  • Smaller babies and premature babies tend to need more sleep, and will be more likely to doze on and off between feeds.

  • Larger babies are capable of staying awake for an hour or so and sleeping for at least one longer spell of four to five hours during a 24-hour period.

  • By the age of one month, most babies who are feeding well and gaining weight (6–8 oz a week) are capable of sleeping for one longer stretch of five to six hours between feeds.

Q **How do I make sure that the longer stretch of sleeping is always in the night and not during the day?**

A • Follow my routines and always start your day at 7:00 A.M., so that you have enough time to fit in all the feeds before 11:00 P.M.

  • Try to keep your baby awake for at least six to eight hours between 7:00 A.M. and 7:00 P.M.

  • Ensure that your baby stays awake for as much of the two-hour social period as possible. Once he is awake a total of eight hours between 7:00 A.M. and 7:00 P.M., he will be more likely to sleep longer in the night.

  • Always distinguish between sleep and awake time. During the first few weeks, put the baby in a dark room for all sleeps.

  • Do not talk to your baby or overstimulate him during the feeds between 7:00 P.M. and 7:00 A.M.

Q **I am trying to stick to your routines, but my four-week-old baby can only stay awake for an hour at the most after feeds. Should I be trying to make him stay awake longer?**

A • If your baby is feeding well and gaining between 6–8 oz per week, sleeping well between feeds in the night, and alert for some of his awake periods during the day, he is just one of those babies who needs more sleep.

  • If he is waking up more than twice in the night or staying awake for over an hour in the night despite feeding well at 11:00 P.M., try stimulating him a bit more during the day.

- While the 11:00 P.M. feed should always be a quiet feed, a baby under three months needs to be awake for 45 minutes. A sleepy feed at this time will most certainly result in a baby being more awake around 2:00–3:00 A.M.
- If you structure your baby's feeds and sleep times between 7:00 A.M. and 11:00 P.M. by my routines, when your baby does cut back his sleep, it will be at the right time.

Q **The routine seems very restricting. If I go out with my four-week-old during waking time he goes straight to sleep in the stroller, which means he has slept too much.**

A • Whether your baby is in my routine or not, during the first couple of months life is restrictive due to the amount of time spent feeding.
- By two months most babies are capable of going longer between feeds and are quicker at feeding. This makes trips easier.
- For the first two months if you plan your trips to fit around his sleep time, by eight weeks he will be able to stay awake longer when you take him out in the car or stroller.

Q **My four-week-old baby has suddenly started to wake up at nine in the evening. If I feed him, then he wakes up twice in the night at 1:00 A.M. and 5:00 A.M. I have tried making him hold out until 10:00 P.M., but then he is so tired he doesn't feed properly, which means he still wakes up earlier.**

A • Around one month the light and deep sleep become much more defined. I find that a lot of babies come into a very light sleep around 9:00 P.M., so ensure that the area around the nursery is not subject to loud, sudden noises and that the baby cannot hear your voice at this time.
- Breast-fed babies may need a small amount of expressed milk after the 6:00 P.M. feed.
- If you have to feed him at 9:00 P.M., try to settle him with one breast or a couple of ounces, then push the 10:30 P.M. feed to 11:30 P.M. Hopefully he will then take a full feed, which would get him through to 3:30 A.M.

Q **I always have to wake my baby of ten weeks for his 10:30 P.M. feed, then he only takes 3–4 oz and wakes again at 4:00 A.M.**

Could I just drop the last feed and see if he goes through until 4:00 A.M. without that feed?

A • I would not advise getting rid of the feed yet, as he could wake up at 1:00 A.M. and then 5:00 A.M., which in effect would be two night wakings. I have always found it best to get the baby sleeping through to 7:00 A.M., and taking solids, before dropping the 11:00 P.M. feed. This usually happens between four and five months.

• Make sure he is tucked in properly; often a baby getting out of his blankets and thrashing around in his light sleep is enough to arouse him to a fully awake state. If he is not getting out of his covers, I would wait 10–15 minutes before going to him, then I would try settling him with some water. If he settles with the water he will make up for the lost feed during the day, and at his age the increased daily milk intake usually has the additional effect of him not needing to feed in the night. If he does not settle with the water, I would try to settle him with a small feed and try again in a couple of weeks.

• If, by the time he reaches four months, he has started solids, but is still waking up, I would be inclined to offer him water for a few nights, then get tough if that did not work. This of course could only be done if your baby was gaining the right amount of weight each week and getting the right amount of milk and food during the day.

Q **My friend's baby of three months does not have a set sleep plan during the day, yet he sleeps well at night and seems very happy. Does it really matter about establishing daytime sleep?**

A • Recent research shows that children up to the age of two years benefit physically and psychologically from a proper structured nap in the middle of the day.

• During the first few months many babies are happy to doze on and off in a car seat or bassinet, which can be very convenient for the parents as it allows them more flexibility. Unfortunately once the baby becomes bigger and more active, he is unlikely to fall asleep happily in the car seat. It can then be very difficult to get him to sleep in his big crib during the day.

• Sleep in a car seat is usually short and of poor quality; as he gets older he will most likely spend most of his day catnapping and become overtired and irritable.

Q My six-month-old baby, who has always slept 45 minutes in the morning, plus a good two hours at lunchtime, now wakes up after one hour and refuses to go back to sleep no matter how long I leave her. She also refuses to take a nap later in the afternoon, which means she is very grumpy for most of the afternoon and needs to go to bed at 6:00 P.M. This is starting to result in earlier and earlier waking times.

A • Check she is not being disturbed by older children playing nearby or by the vacuum cleaner. Make sure that the room is really dark, and that she is tucked in really well.

• Ensure that she is getting enough physical exercise in the morning. At this age she should spend a great deal of her waking time on the floor, rolling and kicking.

• Make sure that she is not going to sleep before 9:00 A.M., and cut back this nap by ten minutes every three days until she ends up with a nap of no more than 20–25 minutes in the morning.

Q At what age do you think a baby can go without a daytime nap?

A • In my experience all babies and young children benefit from properly structured sleep until they are at least two years of age. As they get older they may not need to sleep during the day, but a period of quiet time in their bed is always beneficial to both toddler and mother.

• Most very young babies need three naps a day. The naps should be made up of one long nap and two shorter naps. Between four and six months the baby normally cuts back on the late afternoon nap until he manages to get through to bedtime without it.

• Between the ages of 15 months and 18 months, your baby will show signs of wanting to drop his second nap. You should always encourage it to be the morning nap.

• If he drops the afternoon nap and has a two-hour nap in the morning, he will be exhausted by 6:00 P.M. and go into a very deep sleep at 7:00 P.M. This usually leads to an earlier wake-up time in the morning.

❀ 4 ❀

Feeding in the first year

Breast-feeding

Breast is best and the most natural way to feed your baby, as all the baby experts agree. Some have dedicated complete books on how to do it successfully and the benefits for both mother and baby. Immediately after the birth, midwives and some nurses encourage new mothers to put the baby straight to the breast, and guide them through the techniques of positioning and latching the baby on. There are also organizations that devote themselves totally to promoting breast-feeding and that also provide trained breast-feeding counselors to support and guide mothers who are experiencing difficulties in the early weeks.

According to the American Association of Pediatrics as of 1997, 62.4 percent of mothers are breast-feeding their newborns. Only 26 percent are still doing so after six months.

The most common reasons given by mothers for giving up breast-feeding are:

- a feeling that they are not producing enough milk
- cracked nipples and pain during feeding
- the baby is discontented and not thriving
- exhaustion due to the baby feeding for hours at a time, often throughout the whole night
- they don't enjoy breast-feeding and start to dread feeding times.

I think it is very sad if a mother has to give up for any or all of the first four reasons. If, however, a mother really hates breast-feeding, she should not be pressured into continuing. To quote child-care expert Penelope Leach, "Feeding is only a part of motherhood." Having observed hundreds of mothers over the last ten years, I would like to reassure any mother who absolutely hates breast-feeding that, contrary to some breast-feeding gurus' advice, your baby will not suffer physically or emotionally if you decide to change to formula. The most important thing is that you and your baby are happy with what you are doing, which is very difficult if you dislike breast-feeding. Speaking from personal experience, my own mother only breast-fed me for about ten days, and no one could have bonded more than my mother and me. Equally, I have friends who were breast-fed for nearly two years, and they cannot stand the sight of their mothers! So if you decide breast-feeding is not for you, ignore any criticism, establish bottle-feeding and enjoy your baby. Hundreds of thousands of babies every year all over the world are fed exclusively on formula and grow and thrive happily. The reality is that if "formula" was not a very good substitute for breast-feeding when this is either not possible or not working, it would have been banned by the health authorities years ago.

However, I must stress that contrary to the advice you may get from well-meaning grandmas or aunties, bottle-feeding does not necessarily guarantee you a more contented baby, or make it easier to put your baby into a routine. Whether your baby is breast-fed or bottle-fed, it will still take time and perseverance to establish a routine, so do not change your baby's feeding to formula thinking you will achieve instant results. A bottle-fed baby will need as much guidance and help into a routine as a breast-fed one, the only difference being that all the responsibility normally lies with the mother who is breast-feeding. This is where my breast-feeding routines can give the best of both worlds to mothers who wish to breast-feed, but also want a routine.

I have tried and tested various ways of establishing breast-feeding, and the breast-feeding routine I have devised is without doubt the one that has proved the most successful time and time again. The mothers who follow all my guidelines report that within two weeks a definite pattern of sleeping and feeding has emerged, the baby's weight gain is good and, most importantly, the baby is very happy and content. Before I explain how and why my methods work so well, I will briefly discuss the weak points of other methods I have tried, and why I feel these other methods do not always meet a baby's natural feeding and sleeping needs.

Four hourly routine

Years ago, when hospital birth took over from home birth, women stayed in the maternity unit for up to 10 or 14 days. By the time they left the hospital their babies were often already in a four hourly feeding pattern. Breast-feeding mothers were encouraged to adopt the same pattern as that of the formula-fed babies. The babies were brought to their mothers for feeding every four hours, a strict 10–15 minutes on each breast was allowed, then the babies were taken back to the nursery. If a baby could not manage to go four hours between feeds, the mother was told she was not producing enough milk to feed her baby, and was advised to supplement with formula. I would be a multi-millionaire if I had a pound for every granny who has said to me "My milk dried up the minute I left the hospital." The reality was that, due to rigid routines and restricted timing of feeds, the mother's milk had started to dry up long before she left the hospital. The trend for bottle-feeding became well established in the fifties and sixties with many mothers not even attempting to breast-feed. This trend continued well into the seventies. Then, as research started to discover more and more information regarding the health benefits of breast-feeding, the trend started to swing back to breast-feeding again.

The main reasons why strict four hourly feeding can fail are:

- Six feeds a day in the early days are often not enough to stimulate a good milk supply.
- Babies need to feed little and often in the early days; restricting feeding to six feeds may lead to your baby being short of his daily intake.
- Babies between one week and six weeks usually need at least 30 minutes to reach the hind milk.
- Hind milk is at least three times higher in fat content than fore milk, and is essential for satisfying your baby's hunger.

Demand feeding

The advice given nowadays is to feed your baby on demand. Mothers are encouraged to let their babies take the lead, allowing the baby to feed as often and for as long as he wants. This way you can be sure that your baby's nutritional needs are always met and that he never goes hungry, as each time your baby empties the breast this signals the breasts to make more milk. When they leave the hospital, many babies are feeding up to 10 or 12 times a day. Mothers are reassured that this is normal for the first few weeks, that things will eventually settle down and that the baby will start to go longer between feeds.

While I agree totally that the baby should be frequently put to the breast in the early days to stimulate the breast supply, I think the advice so often given, to let the baby suck as long as he wants, is completely wrong. Some very "sucky" babies would go on for hours, leaving the new mother in agony before breast-feeding has hardly even begun. Time and time again I meet mothers who by the end of the first week of breast-feeding are hating it. The cry is always the same: exhaustion from the baby feeding for hours at a time, and tender, painful nipples. Even worse, the nipples can often become cracked and bleeding, as a result of not positioning the baby correctly on the breast. In my experience you can show a mother repeatedly the correct way to latch the baby on to the breast, but if she gets absolutely exhausted by constant feeding day and night, it is unlikely that she will have the energy to concentrate properly on the correct positioning of the baby on the breast.

As well as being told they should feed their baby on demand, mothers are also advised to get a lot of rest and eat properly. This advice is totally contradictory and virtually impossible to follow, leaving the mother feeling like a total failure at the onset of breast-feeding.

The second problem that I find occurs time and time again when a new mother is "feeding on demand," is that of the sleepy baby. Very often, these are babies born by cesarean. The mother is lulled into a false sense of security; she proudly announces that her baby sleeps and feeds well, often going five to six hours between feeds. By the end of the first week, the mother's milk has come in and balanced out to meet the baby's needs. The reality hits home around the tenth day, when these babies perk up and start to look for more food. The mother then has to resort to feeding little and often to satisfy the baby's needs, which leaves many mothers feeling they are on a backward track. The fact is that it is much easier to get a good milk supply going when the milk first comes in. Yet again the term "demand feeding" is contradictory. It implies that by feeding your baby every time he demands it you can be sure he is getting enough to eat. All too often it is not made clear to the mothers of these sleepy babies that they should be woken every three to four hours to feed. If necessary a little milk should be expressed two or three times a day to encourage a good milk supply, ready for when the baby starts demanding more feeds.

Last but not least, there is yet another very important reason why the term "demand feeding" is used too loosely. It is that it leads new mothers to believe that feeding several times a night is normal. Not structuring a feeding pattern offers no guarantee that the baby will automatically feed more during the day. Again the advice is that the baby will sort itself out, but mothers are not told that with some babies it may take months! All too often I visit mothers whose babies are feeding so much in the night that when they do wake up for feeds during the day, they tend to be short, small feeds. This leads to a vicious circle of the baby needing to feed more in the night to satisfy its daily needs.

The main reasons why demand feeding can fail are:

- The term "demand feeding" is used too literally, and the baby is fed every time it cries. Mothers are not taught to look for other reasons why the baby may be crying, such as overstimulation or overtiredness.
- A baby who continues to feed 10–12 times a day after the first week will very quickly become exhausted through lack of sleep.
- Exhaustion and stress reduce the mother's milk supply, increasing the baby's need to feed little and often.
- Exhaustion leads to the mother being too tired to concentrate properly on positioning the baby correctly on the breast for any length of time.
- Poor positioning on the breast is the main reason for painful, and often cracked and bleeding nipples.
- A sleepy baby left too long between feeds in the early days reduces the mother's chances of building up a good milk supply.

My methods for successful breast-feeding

The key to successful breast-feeding is getting off to the right start. All breast-feeding counselors agree that in order to produce enough milk, it is essential that the breasts are stimulated frequently during the early days. I agree totally with this advice. Years ago, lack of breast stimulation was one of the main reasons breast-feeding failed when a strict four hourly routine was adhered to. It is also the same reason why breast-feeding goes wrong with a very sleepy baby.

Little and often during the first few days is the best way to establish breast-feeding. I advise all my mothers to start off by offering five minutes each side every three hours, increasing the time by a few minutes each day until the milk comes in. Somewhere between the third and fifth day your milk will be in, and you should have increased the baby's sucking time on the breast to 15–20 minutes. Many babies will get enough milk from the first breast, and be content to go three hours before demanding a feed again.

However, if you find your baby is demanding food long before three hours have passed, he should be offered both breasts at each feed. It is absolutely essential that you make sure he has emptied the first breast totally before putting him to the second breast. If you change breasts too soon he will end up getting too much fore milk, which is one of the main causes of babies never seeming satisfied and suffering from colic. It may take a sleepy baby 20–25 minutes to reach the very important

Positioning the baby at the breast

hind milk (which is at least three times fattier than the fore milk) and to empty the breast.

Feeding your baby every three hours will help build up your milk supply much quicker, and if he is fed enough during the day he will be much more likely to go to sleep for longer periods between feeds in the night. It also avoids the mother becoming too exhausted, which is another major factor in breast-feeding going wrong. During the first few days, between 6:00 A.M. and midnight, wake your baby every three hours for short feeds. This will ensure that the feeding gets off to the best possible start, in time for when the milk comes in. As with anything in life, success only comes from building a good foundation. All my mothers who establish every-three-hour feeds in the hospital find that by the end of the first week a pattern has emerged, and then very quickly they can adapt their baby's feeding pattern to my first routine.

The first breast-feeding routine not only helps you establish a good milk supply, but will also enable you to learn all your baby's many different needs: hunger, tiredness, boredom, overstimulation.

The main reasons why my breast-feeding methods are so successful are:

- Waking the baby every three hours in the first few days for shorter feeds allows the mother's nipples to get used to the baby's sucking gradually. This avoids the nipples becoming too painful or, even worse, cracked and bleeding. It will also help ease the pain of engorgement when the milk comes in.
- Feeding little and often will avoid the baby spending hours sucking on an empty breast trying to satisfy his hunger, which often occurs when a baby is allowed to go longer than three hours between feeds in the first week.
- A newborn baby's tummy is tiny, and his daily needs can only be satisfied by feeding little and often. If you feed your baby every three hours between 6:00 A.M. and midnight, the "feeding-all-night syndrome" should never occur. Even a very small baby is capable of going one longer spell in between feeds, and following my advice ensures that this will happen at night, not during the day.
- Successful breast-feeding can only be achieved if a mother feels relaxed and comfortable. This is impossible if, having just given birth, she becomes exhausted from being awake and feeding all night. Stress and exhaustion in the first few weeks are two of the

main reasons why so many mothers give up breast-feeding by the
end of the first month.

- Newborn babies do not know the difference between day and
night. Babies will only learn to associate daytime with feeding
and social activities if they are not allowed to sleep for long periods between feeds from 7:00 A.M. to 7:00 P.M.

- A sleepy baby may not demand to be fed very often in the early
days. This can lead to the mother's breasts not being sufficiently
stimulated. Waking the baby every three hours for even the shortest of feeds will ensure that the breasts are stimulated enough to
encourage a good milk supply.

Milk production

Milk "let-down" reflex

The hormones produced during your pregnancy help prepare your
breasts for the production of milk. Once your baby is born and put to
the breast to suck, a hormone called oxytocin is released from the pi-
tuitary gland at the base of your brain, which sends a "let-down" signal to the breasts. The muscles supporting the milk glands contract, and
the milk is pushed down the 15 or 20 milk ducts as the baby sucks.
Many women feel a slight tingling in their breasts and their womb con-
tracting when their milk lets down. These feelings normally disappear
within a week or two. You may also experience a let-down when you
hear your baby cry, or if you think about him when you are apart. If you
get tense or are very stressed, oxytocin is not released, making it difficult for your milk to let down. Therefore it is essential for successful
breast-feeding that you feel calm and relaxed. This can be helped by
preparing everything needed for a feed in advance. Make sure you are
sitting comfortably with your back straight, and the baby well supported. Take time to position him on the breast correctly. Pain caused
by incorrect positioning also affects oxytocin being released and affects the "let-down" reflex.

Milk composition

The first milk your breasts will produce is called colostrum. It is
higher in protein and vitamins and lower in carbohydrates and fat than

the mature milk that comes in between the third and fifth day. Colostrum also contains some of your antibodies, which will help your baby resist any infections you may have had. Compared to the mature milk that soon follows, colostrum is much thicker and looks more yellow. By the second to third day, the breasts are producing a mixture of colostrum and mature milk. Then somewhere between the third and fifth day the breasts become engorged, and they will feel very hard, tender and often painful to the touch. This is a sign that the mature milk is fully in. The pain is caused not only by the milk coming in, but by the enlargement of the milk glands in the breasts and the increased blood supply to the breasts. When the milk comes in, it is essential to feed your baby little and often. Not only will it help stimulate a good milk supply, but it will help relieve the pain of engorgement. During this time it may be difficult for your baby to latch on to the breast, and it may be necessary to express a little milk before feeding. This can be done by placing warm, wet washcloths on the breasts and gently expressing a little milk by hand.

Mature milk looks very different from colostrum. It is thinner and looks slightly blue in color, and its composition also changes during the feed. At the beginning of the feed your baby gets the fore milk, which is high in volume and low in fat. As the feed progresses, your baby's sucking will slow down and he will pause for longer between sucks. This is a sign that he is reaching the hind milk. Although he only gets a small amount of hind milk, it is very important that he is left on the breast long enough to reach it. It is this hind milk that will help your baby go longer between feeds. If you transfer him to the second breast before he has totally emptied the first breast, he will be more likely to get two servings of fore milk. This will leave him feeling hungry again in a couple of hours. Another feed of fore milk will quickly lead to your baby becoming very "colicky." While some babies do not get enough to eat from only one breast and need to be put on the second breast, always check that he has completely emptied the first breast before transferring him. I find that by the end of the first week, by making sure babies are given at least 25 minutes on the first breast, and offered the second breast for 5–15 minutes, I can be sure that they are getting the right balance of fore milk and hind milk. It also ensures that they are content to go between three and four hours before demanding their next feed. If your baby is feeding from both breasts at each feed, always remember to start the next feed on the breast you last fed from, so that you can be sure that each breast is totally emptied every second feed.

In order to encourage a quick and easy let-down and ensure that your baby gets the right balance of fore milk and hind milk, the following guidelines should be followed:

- Make sure that you rest as much as possible between feeds, and that you do not go too long between meals. Also eat small, healthy snacks between meals.
- Prepare in advance everything needed for the feed: a comfortable chair with arms and a straight back and perhaps a footstool. Cushions to support both you and the baby, a drink of water and some soothing music will all help toward a relaxing, enjoyable feed for both of you.
- It is essential that you take your time to position the baby on the breast correctly; poor positioning leads to painful and often cracked, bleeding nipples. This in turn can affect your let-down and result in a poor feed.
- Always make sure your baby has completely emptied the first breast before putting him on the second. It is the small amount of high-fat hind milk at the end of a feed that will help your baby go longer between feeds.
- Not all babies need the second breast in the early days. If your baby has totally emptied the first breast, burp him and change his diaper, then offer him the second breast. If he needs more he will take it. If not, start him off on that breast at the next feed.
- If your baby does feed from the second breast, you should still start on that breast at the next feed. This will ensure that each breast is totally emptied every second feed, thus signaling the breasts to make more milk.
- Once the milk is in and you have built up the time your baby feeds from the breast, it is important that he is on the breast long enough to completely empty it and reach the hind milk. Some babies need up to 30 minutes to completely empty the breast. By gently squeezing your nipple between your thumb and forefinger, you will be able to check if there is any milk still in the breast.
- **Never, ever, allow your baby to suck on an empty breast. This will only lead to very painful nipples.**

Weaning your baby from the breast to the bottle

However long you have breast-fed, it is important to plan the transition from breast-feeding to bottle-feeding properly. When deciding for how long you intend to breast-feed your baby, you should take into consideration that once you have established a good milk supply, you must allow approximately a week to drop each feed. For example, it can take six weeks to establish a good milk supply, and if you decide to give up breast-feeding, you should allow at the very least a further five weeks to drop all breast-feeds and establish bottle-feeding. This information is very important for mothers who are planning to go back to work. If you give up breast-feeding before you have established a good milk supply, you should still allow enough time for your baby to get used to feeding from the bottle. Some babies can get very upset if they suddenly lose the pleasure and comfort they get from breast-feeding.

For a mother who has breast-fed for less than a month, I generally advise a period of three to four days in between dropping feeds. For a mother who has been breast-feeding longer than a month, it is best to allow five to seven days in between dropping feeds. Assuming that the baby is already on a bottle-feed at 10:00 P.M., the next breast-feed to drop should be at 11:00 A.M. The best way to do this is gradually to reduce the length of time the baby feeds from the breast by five minutes each day and supplement with formula. Once your baby is taking a full bottle-feed, the breast-feed can be dropped. If you plan the weaning carefully from the breast to formula, your baby will have time to adjust to the bottle and you avoid the risk of developing mastitis. This can happen if the milk ducts become blocked due to engorgement—a common problem among mothers who instantly drop a feed.

I suggest that you continue to express at 10:00 P.M. throughout the weaning process. The amount of milk expressed will be an indicator of how quickly your milk supply is going down. Some mothers find that once they are down to two breast-feeds a day, their milk reduces very rapidly. The signs to watch out for are: your baby being irritable and unsettled after a feed or wanting a feed long before it is normally due. If your baby shows either of these signs he should be given 1–2 oz of expressed milk or formula immediately after the breast-feed. This will ensure that his sleeping pattern does not go wrong due to hunger.

The chart on page 62 is a guideline for which feeds to drop first. Each stage represents the period of time between dropping feeds, either three to four days or five to seven days, depending on how long you have been breast-feeding.

Time of feeds	7:00 A.M.	11:00 A.M.	2:30 P.M.	6:30 P.M.	10:30 P.M.
Stage one	Breast	Formula	Breast	Breast	Express*
Stage two	Breast	Formula	Formula	Breast	Express
Stage three	Breast	Formula	Formula	Formula	Express
Stage four	Breast	Formula	Formula	Formula	
Stage five	Formula	Formula	Formula	Formula	

* I recommend that mothers should continue to express at the 10:30 P.M. feed until the baby is three to four months old. This helps maintain a good milk supply, and can be used as an approximate gauge of how much milk they are producing. I find that a mother will usually produce overnight roughly twice the amount she has expressed. When you reach Stage three of the weaning process, the 10:30 P.M. expressing should be dropped gradually, reducing the expressing time by three minutes each night. Once you are only expressing 2 oz and going comfortably through the night, the expressing can be dropped altogether. When the last breast-feed has been dropped, care should be taken not to stimulate the breasts. Sitting in a warm bath with the water covering the breasts helps to get rid of any small amount of milk remaining in the breasts without stimulating them to make more.

Your questions answered

Q   I have very small breasts and am worried that I may not be able to produce enough milk to satisfy my baby's needs.

A   • Breast size is totally irrelevant when it comes to producing breast milk. Each breast, regardless of shape or size, has 15–20 ducts, each duct with its own cluster of milk-making cells. Milk is made within these cells and pushed down the ducts when the baby sucks.

   • During the early days make sure your baby is put to the breast frequently. Most babies need a minimum of eight feeds a day to help stimulate the breasts and establish a good milk supply.

   • Always make sure that your baby totally empties the first breast before putting him on the second breast. This signals the breast to make more milk and also ensures that your baby gets the important hind milk, which is much fattier than the fore milk.

Q **My friend was in agony when her milk came in. Is there anything I can do to help relieve the pain of engorgement?**

A • Put your baby to the breast often and do not let him go longer than three hours during the day between feeds or four to five hours at night.

• A warm bath or warm wet washcloths placed on the breasts before a feed will help the milk flow and, if need be, gently expressing a little milk by hand will make it easier for the baby to latch on.

• Damp washcloths chilled in the fridge and placed on the breasts after a feed will help constrict the blood vessels and reduce the swelling.

• Wear a well-fitting nursing bra that supports your breasts. Make sure that it is not too tight under the arms and does not flatten your nipples.

Q **Many of my friends had to give up breast-feeding because it was so painful.**

A • The main reason women experience pain in the early days is because the baby is not positioned on the breast correctly. The baby ends up chewing on the end of the nipple, causing much pain for the mother, and more often than not resulting in cracked, bleeding nipples and a poor feed for the baby. A pattern soon emerges of the baby needing to feed very quickly again, giving him even more opportunity to damage the nipples.

• Make sure that you always hold your baby with his tummy to your tummy and that his mouth is open wide enough for him to take all of the nipple and as much of the areola as he can manage into his mouth. Apart from ensuring that your baby is well positioned, it is important that you are sitting comfortably. The ideal chair should have a straight back, preferably with arms so that you can position a cushion to support the arm in which you are holding the baby. If you do not support your arm, it will be much more difficult to position and support your baby properly. This can cause him to pull on the breast, which will be painful for you.

Q **I have a three-week-old baby, and I am getting very confused over the conflicting advice. Some people say give both breasts at each feed, others say one is enough.**

A • Be guided by your baby. If he feeds from one breast, is content to go three to four hours between feeds, and is putting on 6–8 oz in weight each week, one breast is obviously enough.

   • If he is looking for food after two hours or is waking up in the night more than once, it would be advisable to offer him the second breast. You may find he only needs the second breast later in the day when your milk supply is at its lowest.

   • Whether your baby has one or two breasts at a feed, always check that the first breast is completely empty before putting him on the second. This can be done by gently squeezing the area around the nipple between your thumb and forefinger.

Q   Do I need to avoid certain foods while breast-feeding?

A • You should continue with the same varied healthy diet that you followed throughout your pregnancy. In addition, you should include small healthy snacks between meals to help keep your energy level up.

   • Ensure that you eat at least 6 oz of either poultry, lean meat or fish. Vegetarians should eat the equivalent in legumes (beans, lentils, split peas, etc.) and grains (wheat, rice, etc.). I have noticed that on the days when some of my breast-feeding mothers did not eat enough protein, their babies were much more unsettled.

   • Some research points to dairy products as the cause of colic in certain babies. If you find your baby develops colic, it may be wise to discuss how to monitor your dairy intake with your pediatrician.

   • Alcohol, artificial sweeteners and caffeine should be avoided. Remember that caffeine is not only found in coffee but also in tea, soft drinks and chocolate. I have found all of these things can upset most babies.

   • Strawberries, tomatoes, mushrooms, onions and fruit juice if taken in large quantities have left many of my babies very irritable. While I do not suggest cutting out all of these from your diet, I would suggest you keep a record of any food or drink consumed 12–16 hours prior to your baby showing signs of tummy ache, explosive bowel movements, excessive gas and crying fits.

   • While working in the Middle and Far East, I observed that breast-feeding mothers followed a much blander diet than normal, and highly spiced foods were omitted. Perhaps it would be wise to avoid spicy foods in the early days.

- Although it is advisable to avoid alcohol, especially spirits, while breast-feeding, some experts advise that a small glass of wine or a dark beer can be beneficial to a mother who is finding it hard to unwind in the evening.

Q   My two-week-old baby wakes up yelling for a feed, only to fall asleep after five minutes on the breast. She then demands to be fed two hours later, leaving me absolutely exhausted.

A - Always make sure your baby is fully awake before you attempt to feed him. Unwrap him in the crib, take his legs out of his pajamas and allow the cool air to get to his skin and give him time to wake up by himself.
- It is very important that sleepy babies are kept cool while feeding. He should not be overdressed, and the room should not be too warm. Have a play mat next to you on the floor, and the minute he gets sleepy, put him on the mat. If necessary remove his clothing, as this will encourage him to stretch and kick. Within a few minutes he will probably protest about being put down, so pick him up and give him a few more minutes on the same breast. This procedure often has to be repeated two or three times. Once he has had 20 minutes on the first breast, burp him well and change his diaper. He can then be put back on the first breast if he has not emptied it, or transferred to the second.
- If you are not using formula at the 10:30 P.M. feed, it is also a good idea to express some milk early in the morning and get your partner to do the 10:00–11:00 P.M. feed. This way you will at least manage to get an uninterrupted few hours sleep for one part of the night.

Bottle-feeding

Many mothers believe if they bottle-feed their babies it will be easier to get them into a routine. The reality is that bottle-feeding alone is no guarantee of a happy, contented baby. A formula-fed baby will need as much guidance into a routine as a breast-fed one. When I do my consultations, I find I have as many bottle-feeding mothers requesting advice as I have breast-feeding mothers. Being woken up several times a night is exhausting, regardless of how you are feeding your baby. The fact that someone else can give a bottle is often quoted as being an advantage, but this can also be possible for a breast-feeding mother who is expressing in the morning. The one real advantage that bottle feeding does have over breast-feeding is that you do not need to worry about what you eat or drink.

If you have decided to bottle-feed, the same routines as for breast-feeding should be followed. The only difference is that you may find your baby is happy to go longer than three hours after the 7:00 A.M. feed, otherwise the timing is exactly the same. In the instances where a feed is being split, such as one breast before the bath and one after, the same pattern applies to bottle-feeding. I would normally make up two separate smaller feeds for this time.

How much and how often

Health authorities advise that a baby under four months would need 2½ oz of milk for each pound of his body weight. A baby weighing around 7 lb would need approximately 18 oz a day. That amount would be divided into six feeds a day. This is only a guideline; hungrier babies may need an extra ounce at some feeds. If your baby is one of these, try to ensure that you structure your feeds so he is taking the bigger feeds at the right time: 7:00 A.M., 10:30 A.M. or 10:30 P.M. If you allow him to get into the habit of having bigger feeds in the middle of the night, it will eventually have the domino effect of him being not so hungry when he wakes in the morning. A vicious circle emerges where he needs to feed in the night because he does not feed enough during the day.

The same guidelines apply as for breast-feeding: aim to get the baby to take most of his daily milk requirements between 7:00 A.M. and 11:00 P.M. This way he will only need a small feed in the middle of the night, and will eventually drop it altogether.

The chart on page 67 is an example of the feeding pattern of one of my babies during his first month. He weighed 7 lb at birth and, with a weekly gain of 6–8 oz, reached just over 9 lb when he was one month old. By structuring the feeding (the bigger feeds at the right times), he was well on the way to dropping his middle-of-the-night feed, and at six weeks he was sleeping through to 6:30 A.M.

Times	7:00 A.M.	10:00–10:30 A.M.	2:00–2:30 P.M.	5:00 P.M.	6:15 P.M.	10:00–11:00 P.M.	2:00–3:00 A.M.	Totals
Week 1	(3 oz)	(3 oz)	(3 oz)	(2 oz)	(2 oz)	(3 oz)	(3 oz)	(19 oz)
Week 2	(3 oz)	(4 oz)	(3 oz)	(3 oz)	(2 oz)	(4 oz)	(3 oz)	(22 oz)
Week 3	(4 oz)	(4 oz)	(3 oz)	(3 oz)	(3 oz)	(4 oz)	(3 oz)	(24 oz)
Week 4	(5 oz)	(4 oz)	(4 oz)	(3 oz)	(3 oz)	(5 oz)	(2 oz)	(26 oz)

N.B. These daily amounts of milk in the chart were calculated to suit that particular baby's specific needs. Remember to adjust the quantities of milk to suit your baby's own needs, but still follow the feeding times of the chart. During growth spurts make sure that the 7:00 A.M., 10:30 A.M., and 10:00–11:00 P.M. feeds are the first to be increased.

Establishing bottle-feeding

When your baby is born, the hospital will provide you with ready-made formula. You may be given a choice of two different brands; both are approved by the health authorities, and there is very little difference in the composition of either milk. The bottles of formula will come with prepackaged sterilized nipples, which are used once and then thrown away. Unless the jars have been stored in the refrigerator, they do not need to be heated; they can be given at room temperature. However, if for some reason you do decide to heat the formula, do so by using either an electric bottle warmer or by standing it in a jug of boiling water.

Never heat up the formula in a microwave, as the heat may not be evenly distributed and you could end up scalding your baby's mouth. Whichever form of heating you use, always test the temperature before giving the bottle to your baby. This can be done by shaking a few drops on the inside of your wrist. It should feel lukewarm, never hot. Once milk is heated, it should never be reheated as this very rapidly increases the bacteria levels in the milk, which is one of the main causes of upset tummies in formula-fed babies.

The advice given in the hospital for formula-fed babies seems to be much the same as that for breast-fed babies: "Feed on demand whenever the baby wants and however much he wants." While you do not have the problem of establishing a milk supply as in breast-feeding, many of the other problems are likely to occur. A bottle-fed baby weighing 7 lb or more at birth could go straight on to the two- to four-week routine. A smaller baby might not manage to last quite as long between feeds and need feedings closer to every three hours.

Ready-made formula is incredibly expensive to use all the time; most parents only use it on trips or in emergencies. Before leaving the hospital, arrange for someone to buy at least two large cans of powdered formula of the same brand as the ready-made milk to which your baby has been introduced at the hospital.

Once home, you will get into a routine of making up in advance the feeds needed for the next 24 hours. When making up the formula, choose a quiet time of the day when you are not too tired and follow the instructions on the can very carefully. Any feeds left over from the previous day should be discarded; likewise never save unfinished bottles. After a bottle has been heated up, it should be used within one hour and any remaining after this time should be thrown out and, if necessary, a fresh bottle heated up. In the early days it is advisable to have an extra bottle of boiled water in the refrigerator, ready for emergencies.

Hygiene and sterilization*

The utmost attention must be paid to hygiene: the sterilizing of all your baby's feeding equipment and the preparation and storing of his formula milk.

The area where you sterilize and prepare your baby's formula should be kept spotlessly clean. Every morning the counter space should be thoroughly washed down with hot soapy water. The cloth used should then be rinsed well under hot running water and the surface wiped again to remove any traces of soap. This should be followed by a final wipe-down using paper towels and antiseptic spray.

The guidelines opposite, if applied to the letter, will reduce the risk of germs, which are so often the cause of tummy upsets in very young babies.

---

* Editor's Note: As mentioned previously, it's common practice in the United States to rigorously sterilize bottles and equipment only for the first three months. After that, wash with hot, soapy water, or run through the dishwasher. Many parents sterilize the water used to mix formula, but ask your pediatrician's advice. If you do choose to sterilize, you'll probably want to make up a full day's supply of bottles at once.

- Surfaces should be washed down thoroughly every day as described above.
- After each feed the bottle and nipple should be rinsed out thoroughly using cold water, and put aside in a bowl ready for washing and sterilizing.
- Get into the habit of sterilizing and preparing formula at the same time every day. Choose a time when you are not too tired and are able to concentrate properly. Most of my mothers find that 12:00 noon, when the baby has gone for his long nap, is a good time.
- Hands should always be washed thoroughly with antibacterial soap under warm running water, then dried with a paper towel, not a dishcloth, which is a breeding ground for germs.
- A separate kettle should be kept for boiling the baby's water; this avoids the water accidentally being boiled a second time if someone wants to make a cup of tea.
- Every day empty the kettle and rinse it out. The water from the tap should be allowed to run for a couple of minutes before filling the kettle.
- Boil the water first, so that it has time to cool while you are washing and sterilizing the bottles.
- Throw away any formula in the refrigerator left over from the previous 24 hours.
- Fill the bowl in which the dirty bottles are stored with hot soapy water. Using a long-handled bottle brush, carefully scrub all the bottles, rims, caps and nipples inside and out. Particular attention should be given to the necks and rims. Then under a hot running tap carefully rinse everything. Wash and rinse the bowl thoroughly, then place all the equipment in the bowl under the running hot water tap. This is to check that everything is thoroughly rinsed—the water should run clear.
- The sterilizer should be rinsed out every day, and the removable parts checked and, if necessary, washed and rinsed. The bottles and nipples should then be packed into the sterilizer following the manufacturer's instructions.
- When the water in the kettle is cool and the bottles sterilized, carefully follow the instructions on the can of formula and make up enough formula for the next 24 hours. In the early days make up an extra bottle of boiled water for emergencies. Once made up, formula should be put immediately into the refrigerator.

Giving the bottle

Prepare everything in advance: chair, cushions, bib and burp cloth. As with breast-feeding, it is important that you are sitting comfortably,

Positioning of your baby while bottle-feeding

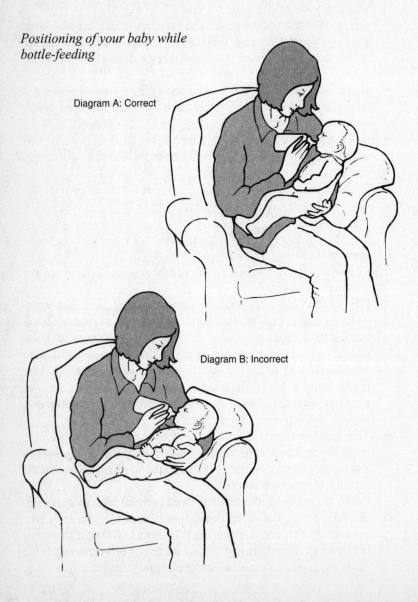

Diagram A: Correct

Diagram B: Incorrect

a similar-type chair should be used, and in the early days I advise all mothers to support the arm in which they are holding the baby with a pillow, which enables you to keep the baby on a slight slope with his back straight. By holding the baby as shown in diagram A (opposite), you will lessen the likelihood of your baby getting air trapped in his tummy if fed as shown in diagram B.

Before starting to feed, loosen and screw the nipple back on; it should be very slightly loose. If it is screwed on too tightly it will not allow air into the bottle, and your baby will end up sucking and not getting any milk.

Check also that the milk is not too hot. It should be just slightly warm. If you get your baby used to very warm milk, you will find that as the feed progresses and the milk gets cool he will refuse to feed. As it is dangerous to reheat the milk or keep the milk standing in hot water for any length of time, you could end up having to heat up two bottles for every feed.

Once feeding, make sure that the bottle is kept tilted up far enough to ensure that the nipple is always filled with milk, to prevent your baby taking in too much air. Allow your baby to drink as much as he wants before stopping to burp him. If you try to burp him before he is ready, he will only get very cross and upset.

Some babies will take most of their feed, burp and then want a break of 10–15 minutes before finishing the remainder of the milk. In the early days, allowing for a break midway, it can take up to 40 minutes to give the bottle. Once your baby is six to eight weeks old, he will most likely finish his feed in about 20 minutes.

If you find your baby is taking a very long time to feed or keeps falling asleep halfway through a feed, it could be because the hole in the nipple is too small. I find that many of my babies have to go straight on to a medium-flow nipple as the slow-flow one is too slow.

For establishing successful bottle-feeding, the following guidelines should be observed:

- Before beginning the feed, check that the ring holding the nipple and the bottle together is very slightly loose; if it is too tight it will restrict the flow of the milk.
- Check that the milk is the right temperature. It should be lukewarm, not hot.
- To avoid gas problems, which are very common among formula-fed babies, always make sure that you are comfortable and holding your baby correctly before beginning the feed.

- Some very young babies need a break in the middle of the feed. Allow up to 40 minutes for your baby to take a full feed.
- If you find you are having always to wake your baby for the 7:00 A.M. feed, only to find he is not so hungry then, cut back the middle-of-the-night feed by 1 oz.
- During growth spurts make sure that you follow the guidelines in the next section. This will avoid your baby cutting back, or even dropping the wrong feeds first.

Structuring milk feeds during the first year

The milk feeding chart on page 79 is structured to fit in with your baby's natural sleep rhythms. It also takes into account that in the first few weeks, regardless of whether babies are breast or formula fed, not all can manage a strict every-four-hour feeding pattern. By two weeks, if your baby has regained his birth weight, he should manage to last three to four hours between feeds. If you follow my routines from birth, you will find that between the second and fourth week most babies are able to last a slightly longer time after one feed. If you structure your baby's feeds, this will automatically happen at the right time: between 11:00 P.M. and 7:00 A.M.

If your baby is not feeding at the times stated on the chart, I would advise you to guide him toward the times appropriate for his age. This can be easily achieved by always starting your day at 7:00 A.M. regardless of the previous night's pattern. Do not expect your baby to suddenly just sleep through one night from 11:00 P.M. to 7:00 A.M. Most babies get through the night by gradually increasing the length of time they sleep after the last feed, over a period of several weeks.

The following extract is from the diary of a mother with a five-week-old baby going approximately four hours between feeds. It shows how quickly things can go wrong, even when a strict every-four-hour routine is followed, if feeds are not structured properly once the baby starts to sleep longer during the night.

Tues.	3:00 A.M.	7:00 A.M.	11:00 A.M.	3:00 P.M.	7:00 P.M.	11:00 P.M.
Wed.	3:00 A.M.	7:00 A.M.	11:00 A.M.	3:00 P.M.	7:00 P.M.	11:00 P.M.
Thurs.	4:00 A.M.	8:00 A.M.	12:00 P.M.	4:00 P.M.	8:00 P.M.	12:00 A.M.
Fri.	5:00 A.M.	9:00 A.M.	1:00 P.M.	5:00 P.M.	9:00 P.M.	11:00 P.M.
Sat.	2:00 A.M.	6:00 A.M.	10:00 A.M.	2:00 P.M.	6:00 P.M.	10:00 P.M.
Sun.	2:00 A.M.	6:00 A.M.	10:00 A.M.	2:00 P.M.	6:00 P.M.	10:00 P.M.

Aware that the feeding pattern was going haywire, the mother tried to get it back on track on the Friday night by waking the baby up at 11:00 P.M. This did not work as the baby had taken a full feed at 9:00 P.M. and was not hungry. It resulted in such a poor feed that the baby woke up at 2:00 A.M. needing a full feed, which meant a total backtrack on night feeding. Even if the mother had managed to settle the baby at 9:00 P.M. with a smaller feed, it is unlikely the baby would have fed any better. The baby had only been asleep for one hour, so it would have been very difficult to wake him up enough to feed properly.

As I mentioned earlier, the easiest way to keep your baby on track with his feeding is always to wake him at 7:00 A.M. Once he is sleeping to 5:00 A.M. or 6:00 A.M., he should be offered a small feed at 7:00 A.M. or 7:30 A.M. This method will not only keep the rest of your feeds on track, but ensure that your baby's sleeping is kept on track as well, and that he is ready to go to bed at 7:00 P.M. The following advice will also ensure that your baby sleeps through the night as soon as he is physically able, and prepare him for the introduction of solids and the eventual reduction of milk feeds.

The 6:00 A.M.–7:00 A.M. feeding

Depending on what time he fed in the night, your baby will probably wake up between 6:00 A.M. and 7:00 A.M., but he should always be woken at 7:00 A.M. regardless. If he had a full feeding at or before 6:00 A.M., he will need a little formula by 7:30 A.M., to keep his feeding and sleeping times on track. Once he is sleeping through the night, he should be the hungriest at this feeding. During growth spurts, breast-fed babies should be fed longer on the second breast, or if you are expressing at 6:45 A.M. reduce this by 1 oz. Bottle-fed babies should have their feedings increased by 1 oz when they are regularly draining their bottle.

By seven months

If your baby is eating a full breakfast of cereal, fruit and perhaps some small pieces of toast, you should aim to cut back the amount of milk fed to him from the bottle. Try to divide his 8 oz feed so that half is given with the cereal and half as a drink. Offer him his drink first at this meal. If you are still breast-feeding, offer one breast, then the solids and finally the other breast. Your baby still needs a minimum of 21 oz a day inclusive of milk used in cooking or on cereal, divided between three to four milk feeds.

By seven to ten months

Introduce a cup at breakfast when your baby is happy to take 4–5 oz from a cup.

By ten months

Try to encourage your baby to take all his milk from a cup. Ensure that you still offer milk at the start of the meal. Once he has taken a couple of ounces of milk, offer him some cereal. Then offer the milk again. It is important that he has at least 6–8 oz of milk divided between his cup and his breakfast cereal. Your baby needs a minimum of 18 oz a day inclusive of milk used in cooking or on cereal, divided between two or three milk feeds.

The 10:00 A.M.–11:00 A.M. feeding

Once your baby is sleeping through or taking only a small feed in the night, he should have the biggest feeding of the day at 7:00 A.M. (as discussed above). If he feeds well, he should be happy to last until 11:00 A.M. before needing another feeding. However, if you feed him before he really needs it, he may not feed well and as a result he may sleep poorly at his lunchtime nap. This will have a domino effect so that each subsequent feeding and nap has to be given earlier and may result in the baby waking up at 6:00 A.M. or earlier the following morning.

This feed would be the next one to be increased during growth spurts.

By five to six months

When your baby is eating some cereal at breakfast, you can start to make this feed later, eventually settling around 12:00 noon. This will set the pattern for three meals a day. As you gradually increase his solids, he will cut back on this feed.

By six to seven months

When your baby is on a proper balanced diet, which includes protein with his lunch, this feed would be replaced with a drink of water or well-diluted juice from a cup. Give him most of his solids before the milk so he does not fill up with liquid first.

Milk given with a protein meal can reduce the iron absorption by up to 50 percent.

The 2:30 P.M. feeding

I recommend that you make this feeding smaller so that your baby feeds really well at the 6:00–7:00 P.M. feeding. If for some reason the baby fed badly at the previous feeding, you should increase this feeding accordingly so that he maintains his daily milk quota.

If your baby is very hungry and regularly drains his bottle at this feeding, then you can give him the full amount, but make sure that he does not take less at the 6:00–7:00 P.M. feeding. For breast-fed babies allow longer on the second breast if they are not getting through to the 6:00–7:00 P.M. feeding happily.

By six to seven months

When your baby is having three full meals a day and his lunchtime milk feed has been replaced with water or well-diluted juice, you will probably need to increase this feed so he is getting his daily milk quota in three feedings. He still needs a minimum of 21 oz a day inclusive of milk used on breakfast cereal.

By nine to ten months

If he starts to lose interest in his morning or evening feeding, you could cut right back on this feeding. If he is getting 18 oz of milk a day (inclusive of milk used in cooking and on cereal) plus a full balanced diet of solids, you could cut this feeding out altogether.

The 6:00–7:00 P.M. feeding

It is important that your baby always has a good feeding at this time if you want him to settle well between 7:00 P.M. and 11:00 P.M. He should not be fed milk after 3:15 P.M. as it could put him off taking a really good feeding at this time. I advise that in the first few weeks this feeding is split between 5:00 P.M. and 6:00 P.M. so that the baby is not too frantic during his bath. Breast-fed babies not settling at 7:00 P.M. should be offered an ounce of expressed milk.

By four to five months

Most babies drop their late feeding by this stage, so this feeding will be the last one of the day. As a consequence you should ensure that it is an adequate one. A baby on solids should still be given most of his milk before the solids, as milk is still the most important form of nutrition at this age.

Most babies would be taking at least 7–8 oz of formula at this age, and a breast-fed baby would need to be fed from both breasts.

If he cuts back or plays during this feeding, then cut right back on his 2:30 P.M. feeding.

By six to seven months

Most babies will now be having a snack at 5:00 P.M. followed by a 7–8 oz bottle or both breasts at 6:30 P.M. If your baby starts to take less at this feeding and is waking up earlier in the morning, go back to giving him the milk first at 6:00 P.M. followed by the solids. Continue this for a couple of weeks before trying the solids at 5:00 P.M. again.

By ten to twelve months

Start encouraging your baby to take some of this feeding from a cup now, so that by one year old he is happy to take all of his last feeding from a cup.

The 10:00–11:00 P.M. feeding

If you always increase the day feedings during your baby's growth spurts, he will probably never require more than 6 oz at this feeding. Breast-fed babies should be encouraged to empty both breasts at this feed. A totally breast-fed baby under three months who wakes up before 3:00 A.M. may need a small amount of expressed milk or formula.

By three to four months

Most bottle-fed babies will be taking 7–8 oz a feeding four times a day and will only want a small feeding of 4–6 oz at this time of night. If your baby is totally breast-fed and is still waking up in the night, despite being weaned and supplemented with expressed milk at the late feeding, it may be worthwhile replacing the late breast-feed with a bottle feed. Some babies simply refuse this feed at three to four months. If your baby is taking 21 oz a day, you can just drop this feeding. If your baby is still feeding at 11:00 P.M. and has slept through the night until 7:00 A.M. for at least two weeks, then I recommend that you bring this feeding forward by ten minutes every three nights, until your baby is sleeping from 10:00 P.M. to 7:00 A.M.

By four to five months

When you have been regularly feeding your baby with rice cereal at the 6:00 P.M. feeding, you should gradually cut back this last feeding. If you do not do this, your baby will not feed so well in the morning.

With bottle-fed babies, cut back this feeding by 1 oz every three nights. With fully breast-fed babies cut back feeding time by two minutes each side. If your baby continues to sleep through on a 2 oz bottle-feed or three minutes on each breast for a further three nights, you should find that you can drop this feeding without him waking during the night.

The 2:00 A.M.–3:00 A.M. feeding

Newborn babies need to feed little and often, and most will wake up sometime between 2:00 A.M. and 3:00 A.M. during the first few weeks. A newborn baby should never be allowed to go longer than three to four hours between feedings during the day, and no longer than four to five hours during the night. Once your baby has regained his birth weight and has a regular weight gain of 6–8 oz each week, you can wait until he wakes in the night.

By four to six weeks

Most babies weighing over 7 lb at birth and gaining a regular 6–8 oz each week are capable of lasting a longer stretch between feedings during the night, as long as:

a) The baby is definitely over 9 lb in weight and taking his daily allowance of milk in the five feeds between 7:00 A.M. and 11:00 P.M.

b) The baby is not sleeping more than four hours between 7:00 A.M. and 7:00 P.M.

By six to eight weeks

If your baby is over 9 lb in weight and gaining 6–8 oz each week, but is still waking between 2:00 A.M. and 3:00 A.M., I recommend that you try to settle him with some water. He will probably wake up again around 5:00 A.M., at which time you can give him a full feeding, followed by a small amount at 7:00–7:30 A.M. This will keep him on track with his feeding and sleep pattern for the rest of the day. Within a week I normally find that babies are sleeping until 4:30–5:00 A.M., gradually increasing their sleep time until 7:00 A.M.

By eight to ten weeks

If your baby is bottle-fed, weighs over 12 lb and is gaining 6–8 oz each week, but persists in waking regularly before 5:00 A.M., I suggest that you wait 15–20 minutes before going to him. Babies of this age often wake out of habit and not hunger, and if left will settle themselves back to sleep. If after three to four days he refuses to settle, it is easier all around to feed him, but do try again a couple of weeks later.

A totally breast-fed baby may genuinely need one feeding in the night up to the age of four months. If, however, you find that you are feeding your baby in the night but he starts to refuse to feed at 7:00 A.M., then you can assume that he is cutting out a feed of his own accord. Therefore, it would be best to take the same approach as with a bottle-fed baby and see if he will settle himself, otherwise you may find that he cuts out the 7:00 A.M. feeding instead of the middle-of-the-night feeding.

By three to four months

Both breast-fed and bottle-fed babies should be able to go one long spell during the night. If your baby insists on waking up in the night and will not settle without feeding, I would try the method Richard Ferber suggests (see further reading at the back of the book). If you gradually dilute the middle-of-the-night feeding with water a little more every few nights, your baby will increase his daytime intake of milk. This would reduce any genuine need for milk in the night. Most babies of this age need approximately 30 oz a day between 7:00 A.M. and 11:00 P.M. to get through the night. If your baby weighs over 14 lb and is drinking in excess of this, he may need to be weaned early. You should discuss this with your pediatrician.

By four to five months

If, when he reaches nearly five months and is weaned, your baby still persists in waking up in the night, it would be wise to consider a sleep training program before a long-term sleep problem evolves.

Milk feeding chart for the first year

2–4 weeks	2:00–3:00 A.M.	6:00–7:00 A.M.	10:00–10:30 A.M.	2:00–2:30 A.M.	5:00 P.M.	6:00–6:30 P.M.	10:00–11:00 P.M.
4–6 weeks	3:00–4:00 A.M.	6:00–7:00 A.M.	10:30–11:00 A.M.	2:00–2:30 P.M.	5:00 P.M.	6:00–6:30 P.M.	10:00–11:00 P.M.
6–8 weeks	4:00–5:00 A.M.	7:30 A.M.	10:45–11:00 A.M.	2:00–2:30 P.M.		6:00–6:30 P.M.	10:00–11:00 P.M.
8–10 weeks	5:00–6:00 A.M.	7:30 A.M.	11:00 A.M.	2:00–2:30 P.M.		6:00–6:30 P.M.	10:00–11:00 P.M.
10–12 weeks	7:00 A.M.	11:00 A.M.	2:00–2:30 P.M.	6:00–6:30 P.M.		10:00–11:00 P.M.	
3–4 months	7:00 A.M.	11:00 A.M.	2:00–2:30 P.M.	6:00–6:30 P.M.		10:00–10:30 P.M.	
4–5 months	7:00 A.M.	11:00 A.M.	2:00–2:30 P.M.	6:00–6:30 P.M.		10:00 P.M.	
5–6 months	7:00 A.M.	11:30 A.M.	2:00–2:30 P.M.	6:00–6:30 P.M.			
6–7 months	7:00 A.M.	2:00–2:30 P.M.	6:00–6:30 P.M.				
7–8 months	7:00 A.M.	2:00–2:30 P.M.	6:00–6:30 P.M.				
8–9 months	7:00 A.M.	2:00–2:30 P.M.	6:00–6:30 P.M.				
9–10 months	7:00 A.M.	5:00 P.M.	6:30–7:00 P.M.				
10–12 months	7:00 A.M.	5:00 P.M.	6:30–7:00 P.M.				

❀ 5 ❀

Routines for the
first year

Benefits for your baby

The dozens and dozens of baby care books I have read are all in agreement in one regard: that in the first few weeks it is impossible to put a small baby into a routine. The implication is that if you even attempt to put your baby on a routine you could seriously damage him. Having successfully spent many years teaching parents how to put their newborns into a routine that results in a happy, thriving, contented baby, I can only assume that the authors of these books have not personally worked with enough babies to know that it is possible.

Parents are always amazed at how easily their baby fits into my routine. Many assume that having a baby on a routine can only be achieved by leaving him to yell until the next feeding, or by leaving him to cry himself to sleep. While this is often the case with the old-fashioned every-four-hour feeding pattern, nothing could be further from the truth with my routines.

These routines are created to meet the natural sleep and feeding needs of all healthy, normal young babies. They also allow for the fact that some babies need more sleep than others, and some may be able to go longer between feedings than others. The basis of these routines evolved over years of observing babies in my care. Some babies would develop a feeding pattern very quickly with little prompting, while others would be difficult to feed and settle for many weeks.

The main observations I made from the babies who settled quickly into a pattern were:

- The parents had a positive approach and tried to keep the first couple of weeks as calm as possible.
- Handling of the baby by visitors was kept to a minimum, so that the baby felt relaxed and secure in his new surroundings.
- The baby always had regular sleep times in the dark in his nursery.
- The baby was kept awake for a short spell after the daytime feeds.
- When awake, he was stimulated and played with by the parents.
- He was bathed at the same time every evening, then fed, and settled in the dark in his nursery.

Benefits for you

By following my routines you will soon learn whether your baby is crying from hunger, tiredness or boredom. The fact that you are able to understand his needs and meet them quickly and confidently, will leave both you and your baby calm and reassured. The usual situation of fretful baby and fraught mother is avoided.

The other big plus for parents following my routines is that they have free time in the evening to relax and enjoy each other's company. This is usually not possible for parents of demand-fed babies, who seem to be at their most fretful between 6:00 P.M. and 10:00 P.M., and require endless rocking and patting.

Establishing a routine

Most young babies can stay awake for up to two hours. If your baby stays awake for longer than two hours, he will become so exhausted that he will need a much longer sleep at his next nap time. This would alter the rest of his routine, resulting in poor evening and nighttime sleep. Therefore it is essential that you structure the two hourly awake period properly, so that the feeding and sleeping plan works well.

Babies learn by association. It is very important that from day one he learns the right associations, and to differentiate between feeding, playing, cuddling and sleeping.

Feeding

Small babies spend a great deal of their waking time feeding. In order to avoid excessive night feeding, it is important to structure and establish a good daytime feeding pattern.

A breast-fed baby needs at least three hours to digest a full feeding, and a bottle-fed baby needs three and a half to four hours. If you feed him before he really needs it, it is very likely that he will only take an ounce or two and will need feeding again in a couple of hours. This can lead to demand feeding, which is more likely to cause a buildup of gas in his digestive tract. Do not let him cry excessively before a feeding as this can also cause gas. Do not overstimulate or distract him while feeding as he will lose interest after a couple of ounces. Avoid talking on the telephone for long periods while feeding. It is important that you concentrate and ensure that your baby eats well. He should always be fed in a position where his back is straight. Do not rock him, as he will think it is sleep time, and if he is sleepy while feeding he will be more likely to vomit.

Playing

All babies love to be cuddled, talked to and sung to. Research also shows that even very small babies like to look at simple books and interesting toys. Babies also need the chance to exercise their muscles. They should be given the chance to kick and move their arms and head while lying on their stomachs. They should also kick on their backs under a play gym.

For your baby to enjoy these things it is important that you do them at the right time. The best time is usually approximately one hour after he is awake and not hungry. He should never be played with or over-stimulated 20 minutes prior to his nap.

Cuddling

Babies need lots of cuddling, but it should always be done when your baby needs it, not when *you* need it. A baby needs energy to grow so it is important that you do not overhandle his small body and exhaust him. While all babies need to be nurtured, they are not toys; satisfy his needs, not your own. Differentiate the type of cuddle during his play-time from that of wind-down time. Wind-down cuddling should have no eye contact, just closeness of bodies. It is important that your baby is not cuddled to sleep while feeding. After one hour of being awake and fed, he should be happy to spend a little time amusing himself; if you constantly cuddle him during playtime, he will be less likely to respond to the cuddles that would normally help settle him for his nap. When cuddling him during the wind-down time, do not talk and avoid eye contact, as it can overstimulate him and result in him becoming overtired and not settled.

Sleep

It is essential for your baby's mental and physical development that he gets enough sleep; without the right amount of sleep your baby will become irritable, fretful and inconsolable.

Along with the routines the following hints will help your baby develop healthy sleeping habits.

- Try to keep him awake for a short spell after his daytime feedings.
- Do not let him sleep too long in the late afternoon.
- Do not feed him after 3:15 P.M., as it will put him off his night feeding.
- Follow the same routine every evening; do not allow visitors in the nursery during wind-down time.
- Do not let him get overtired; allow at least one hour for the bath, feed and wind-down time.
- Do not overstimulate him or play with him after his bath.
- Do not rock him to sleep in your arms; try to settle him in his cot before he goes into a deep sleep.
- If you use a pacifier to wind him down, remove it before you put him in his crib.
- If he falls asleep on the breast or bottle, arouse him slightly before settling him in his crib.

Crying

Obviously all new parents are anxious to make their newborn baby's introduction to the world a happy one. As we all associate crying with pain or unhappiness I can understand why, as a new parent, you will be prepared to do virtually anything to stop your baby crying. A newborn baby's only way of communicating is by crying, and it is important that you do not fall into the trap of thinking the only way of dealing with crying is by feeding your baby.

Listed below are the main reasons a healthy baby would cry. Use it as a checklist to eliminate the possible causes for your baby crying, so you can satisfy his real needs. (See also pages 40–41.)

Hunger

This is most likely to happen in the evening if you have not established a good milk supply. Try resting in the afternoon for a short spell to help increase your milk for the evening feeding. Try offering your baby a small amount of expressed milk until you increase your milk supply.

Tiredness

Babies under six weeks tend to get tired after one hour of being awake. Although they may not be quite ready to sleep, they need to be kept quiet and calm.

Overtiredness

No baby under three months should be allowed to stay awake for more than two hours at a time, as they can become very overtired and impossible to settle. If your baby is fretful two hours after his feeding or from the time he wakes up, he should be calmed down and encouraged to sleep, even if he does not look tired. Overtiredness is one of the main reasons young babies do not sleep well.

Boredom

Even a newborn baby needs to be awake some of the time. Encourage him to be awake for a short spell after his day feeds. Babies under one month love to look at anything black and white, especially pictures of faces.

Gas

All babies take a certain amount of air while feeding, bottle-fed babies more so than breast-fed ones. Given the opportunity, most babies bring up their gas easily. If you suspect that your baby's crying is caused by gas, check that you are allowing enough time between feedings. I have found overfeeding and demand feeding to be the main causes of colic in young babies. A breast-fed baby needs at least three hours to digest a full feeding, and a formula-fed baby should be allowed three and a half to four hours.

Daytime sleep

To ensure good nighttime sleep for your baby, it is essential that you structure his daytime sleep. Too much daytime sleep can result in nighttime wakings. Too little daytime sleep can result in an overtired, irritable baby who has difficulty settling himself to sleep, and who falls asleep only when he is totally exhausted. Infant sleep expert Marc Weissbluth (see page 41) has done extensive research into the nap patterns of more than 200 children. He says that napping is one of the health habits that sets the stage for good overall sleep and explains that a nap offers the baby a break from stimuli and allows him to recharge for further activity. Charles Schaefer Ph.D., professor of psychology at Fairleigh Dickinson University in Teaneck, New Jersey, supports this and says: "Naps structure the day, shape both the baby's and the mother's moods, and offer the only opportunity for Mom to relax or accomplish a few tasks."

Several leading experts on child care are in agreement that naps are essential to a baby's brain development. John Herman Ph.D., infant sleep expert and associate professor of psychology and psychiatry at the University of Texas, says: "If activities are being scheduled to the detriment of sleep, it's a mistake. Parents should remember that everything else in a baby's life should come after sleeping and eating." I would agree totally with this new research and could have confirmed their findings years ago, down to the very times they suggest babies should take their naps.

By three to four months most babies are capable of sleeping 12 hours at night, provided their daytime sleep is no more than three to three and a half hours, divided between two or three naps a day. If you want your baby to sleep from 7:00–7:30 P.M. to 7:00–7:30 A.M., it is very important that you structure these naps so that he has his longest nap at midday, with two shorter ones: one in the morning and one late afternoon. While it may be more convenient to let your baby have a longer nap in the morning followed by a shorter nap in the afternoon, this can lead to problems as he gets older.

Once he reduces his daytime sleep naturally, he is most likely to cut back on his late afternoon nap. His longest nap of the day would then be in the morning. By late afternoon he will be exhausted and need to go to bed by 6:30 P.M. This can confuse the routine, which results in him waking up at 6:00 A.M. If you manage to get him to have a nap in the late afternoon, you could then be faced with the problem of him not settling well at 7:00–7:30 P.M.

Morning nap

Most babies are ready for a nap approximately two hours from the time they wake up in the morning. This should always be a short nap, around 45 minutes to one hour. Between 12 and 18 months they may reduce the time of the nap or cut it out altogether. You will know your baby is ready to drop this nap when he starts taking a long time to settle, and ends up only sleeping 10–15 minutes of his 45-minute nap. If this continues for a couple of weeks and he manages to get through to his lunchtime nap happily, cut out the morning nap altogether. It is very important that you always start to wake him up after the 45-minute period, even if he has only slept for ten minutes. If you allow him to sleep past this time, you will not know whether he is ready to drop the nap. It could also cause him to sleep too little at his lunchtime nap, which could result in the problems that I discussed earlier.

Six weeks onward

Never allow your baby to sleep more than 45 minutes, as it may result in a shorter lunchtime nap. This will affect the rest of his sleep, resulting in an early morning waking. Until a proper sleep pattern has been established, try to ensure that this nap takes place in his nursery, in the dark, with the door shut. Once a proper daytime routine has been established, this nap could at times be taken in the stroller or car seat if you have to go out, but do remember to wake him after the 45 minutes.

Six months onward

If your baby is on three meals a day, this nap may be pushed to 9:30 A.M. You will know your baby is ready for this if he consistently and continually chatters for 30 minutes or so when you put him down. This nap may need to be cut back 20–30 minutes if he is sleeping less than two hours at lunchtime from 12 months onward.

If he is awake at 7:00 A.M., he may still need a short nap of 30 minutes at 9:30 A.M. If you find he is only sleeping 10–15 minutes out of the 45-minute nap time and is getting through happily to his lunchtime nap, you could cut it out altogether. If he sleeps to 8:00 A.M., he should be able to get through to his lunchtime nap, without the morning nap.

Lunchtime nap

This should always be the longest nap of the day. By establishing a good lunchtime nap, you will ensure that your baby is not too tired to enjoy afternoon activities, and that bedtime is relaxed and happy. Recent research shows that a nap between noon and 2:00 P.M. is deeper and more refreshing than a later nap because it coincides with the baby's natural dip in alertness. As I explained earlier, allowing a longer nap in the morning, followed by a shorter nap at this time, will in turn affect the rest of his sleep, which can result in an early morning awakening.

Most babies will need a sleep of two to two and a half hours until they are two years of age, when it will gradually reduce to one to one and a half hours. By three years of age they may not need a nap after lunch, but they should always be encouraged to have some quiet time in their room. Otherwise, they are likely to get very hyperactive by late afternoon, which can affect the night sleep.

Six weeks onward

If your baby is sleeping the full 45 minutes in the morning, he should be woken after 2¼ hours. If for some reason his morning nap was much shorter, then you could allow him 2½ hours. If your baby develops a problem with his nighttime sleep, do not make the mistake of letting him sleep longer during the day.

Six months onward

If your baby is on three meals a day or you have moved the morning nap from 9:00 A.M. to 9:30 A.M., he will most likely need to adjust the lunchtime nap to 12:30 P.M.–2:30 P.M. If he is sleeping less than two hours at lunchtime, check that his morning nap between 7:00 A.M. and 12:00 noon is no more than 45 minutes.

Twelve months onward

If your baby has difficulty in settling for the nap or is waking up after one to one and a half hours, you might have to cut the morning nap right back or cut it out altogether. Do not let him sleep after 2:30 in the afternoon if you want him to go to sleep at 7:00 P.M.

Late-afternoon nap

This is the shortest nap of the three, and the one the baby should drop first. It is not essential that your baby goes in his crib for this nap. It is a good idea occasionally to let him catnap in his stroller or chair for this nap, as it allows you the freedom to get out and about.

Three months onward

If you want your baby to go to sleep at 7:00 P.M., he should never sleep more than 45 minutes at this nap, and he should always be awake by 5:00 P.M. regardless of how long or short his sleep was. Most babies who are sleeping well at the other two naps will gradually cut back on this sleep until they cut it out altogether. If for some reason his lunchtime nap was cut short, you would need to allow him a short sleep now, but ensure that the daily total does not exceed the amount needed for his age.

Adjusting the routines

Birth to four months

I have tried many different routines over the years, and without exception I have found the 7:00 A.M. to 7:00 P.M. routine to be the one in which tiny babies and young infants are happiest. It fits in with their natural sleep rhythms and their need to feed little and often. I urge parents to try and stick to the original routine whenever possible. Once your baby reaches the age of four months, is on four feeds a day and needs less sleep, it is possible to change the routine without affecting your baby's natural needs for the right amount of sleep and number of feeds.

Up to the age of four months, the following points should be noted when planning a routine:

- In the very early weeks to avoid more than one waking in the night, you must fit in at least five feedings before midnight. This can only be done if your baby starts his day at 6:00 A.M. or 7:00 A.M.
- An 8:00 A.M. to 8:00 P.M. routine in the first few weeks would mean your baby would end up feeding twice between midnight and 7:00 A.M.

Four months onward

From four months most babies who have started solids will have dropped their late night feed. It is then easier to adjust the routine. If your baby has been sleeping regularly to 7:00 A.M. it could be possible to change to a 7:30 A.M. or 8:00 A.M. start, and push the rest of the routine forward. Your baby would obviously need to go to sleep later in the evenings. If you want your baby to sleep later but still go to bed at 7:00 P.M., try the following:

- Cut right back on the morning nap, so that your baby is ready to go to bed at 12:00–12:30 P.M.
- Allow a nap of no longer than two hours at lunchtime and no late afternoon nap.

Out and about

In the first few weeks most young babies will go to sleep the minute they are in the car or the stroller. If possible, try to organize shopping trips during the sleep times so that the routine is not too disrupted. Once the routine is established and your baby is nearer eight weeks, you will find that you are able to go out more without him falling asleep the whole time.

If you are planning a day visit to friends, depending on the length of the visit, you can usually work it into the routine by traveling between 9:00 A.M. and 10:00 A.M. or 1:00 P.M. and 2:00 P.M. By the time you arrive at the destination, the baby will be due for a feeding and can be kept awake. Likewise, by making the return journey between 4:00 P.M. and 5:00 P.M. or after 7:00 P.M., you should manage to keep things on track.

In the early days a lunchtime nap may sometimes go wrong, and your baby will refuse to go back to sleep. Obviously he cannot make it through from 1:00 P.M. to 4:00 P.M. happily. I find the best way to deal with this is to allow 30 minutes after the 2:30 P.M. feed, then a further 30 minutes at 4:30 P.M. This should stop him from getting overtired and irritable and get things back on track so that he goes to sleep well at 7:00 P.M.

Sleep required during the first year

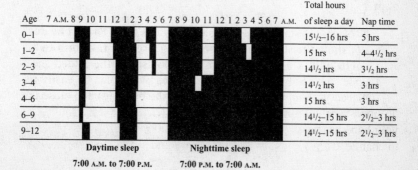

Age	7 A.M. 8 9 10 11 12 1 2 3 4 5 6 7 8 9 10 11 12 1 2 3 4 5 6 7 A.M.	Total hours of sleep a day	Nap time
0–1		15½–16 hrs	5 hrs
1–2		15 hrs	4–4½ hrs
2–3		14½ hrs	3½ hrs
3–4		14½ hrs	3 hrs
4–6		15 hrs	3 hrs
6–9		14½–15 hrs	2½–3 hrs
9–12		14½–15 hrs	2½–3 hrs

Daytime sleep
7:00 A.M. to 7:00 P.M.   Nighttime sleep
7:00 P.M. to 7:00 A.M.

Routine for a breast-feeding baby
at two to four weeks

Feeding times	Nap times between 7:00 A.M. and 7:00 P.M.
7:00 A.M.	8:30–9:00 A.M. to 10:00 A.M.
10:00 A.M.	11:30–12:00 noon to 2:00 P.M.
2:00 P.M.	4:00–5:00 P.M.
5:00 P.M.	
6:15 P.M.	
10:30 P.M.	**Maximum daily sleep five hours**

EXPRESSING TIMES: 6:45 A.M., 9:45 A.M. AND 10:00 P.M.

7:00 A.M.

- **Baby should be awake, diaper changed and feeding no later than 7:00 A.M.**
- He needs 20–25 minutes on the full breast, then 10–15 minutes on the second breast after you have expressed 2–3 oz.
- If he fed at 5:00 A.M. or 6:00 A.M., offer 20–25 minutes from the second breast after expressing 3 oz.
- **Do not feed after 7:45 A.M., as it will put baby off his next feed.** He can stay awake for up to two hours.

8:00 A.M.

- You should have cereal, toast and a drink no later than 8:00 A.M.

8:45 A.M.

- Baby should start to get a bit sleepy by this time. **Even if he does not show the signs, he will be getting tired, so take him to his room now.** Check his diaper and draw sheet (the folded sheet under his head meant to catch dribbles, which can be easily replaced without disturbing the rest of the bedding) and close the curtains.

9:00 A.M.

- **Before he is asleep or before he goes into a deep sleep, settle baby in his crib, fully swaddled (see page 24), in the dark with the door shut, no later than 9:00 A.M.** He needs a sleep of no longer than 1½ hours.
- Wash and sterilize bottles and expressing equipment.

9:45 A.M.

- Open the curtains and unswaddle baby so that he can wake up naturally.
- Prepare things for sponge bath and dressing.

10:00 A.M.

- **Baby must be fully awake now, regardless of how long he slept.**
- He should be given 20–25 minutes from the breast he last fed on while you drink a large glass of water.
- Wash and dress baby, remembering to cream all his creases.

10:30 A.M.

- Express 2 oz from the second breast, then offer baby 10–15 minutes. **Do not feed after 11:15 A.M., as it will put him off his next feed.**
- Lay him on his play mat so that he can play before he gets too tired.

11:30 A.M.

- If baby was very alert and awake during the previous two hours, he may start to get tired by 11:30 A.M. and would need to be in bed by 11:45 A.M.

11:45 A.M.

- Regardless of what he has done earlier, he should now be taken to his room.
- Check the draw sheet and change his diaper.

- Close the curtains and **settle baby once he is drowsy, fully swaddled and in the dark with the door shut, no later than 12:00 noon.**

11:30–12:00 noon to 2:00 P.M.

- Baby needs a nap of no longer than 2½ hours from the time he went down.
- If he slept 1½ hours earlier, only allow him two hours this nap time.
- **If he wakes up after 45 minutes, check the swaddle, but do not talk to him or turn the lights on.**
- **Allow 20 minutes for him to resettle himself;** if he's still unsettled, offer him half his 2:00 P.M. feed and try to settle him back to sleep until 2:00 P.M.

12:00 noon

- Wash and sterilize expressing equipment, then you should have lunch and rest before the next feed.

2:00 P.M.

- **Baby must be awake and feeding no later than 2:00 P.M. regardless of how long he has slept.**
- Open the curtains, unswaddle him and allow him to wake up naturally. Change his diaper.
- Give 20–25 minutes from the breast he last fed on. If he is still hungry, offer 10–15 minutes from the other breast while you drink a large glass of water.
- **Do not feed after 3:15 P.M., as it will put him off his next feed.**
- **It is very important that he is fully awake now until 4:00 P.M., so he goes down well at 7:00 P.M.**—if he was very alert in the morning he may be more sleepy now. Do not put too many clothes on him, as extra warmth will make him drowsy.
- Lay him on his play mat and encourage him to play.

4:00 P.M.

- Change baby's diaper. This is a good time to take him for a walk to ensure that he sleeps well, and is refreshed for his bath and next feed.
- **Baby should not sleep after 5:00 P.M. if you want him to go down well at 7:00 P.M.**

5:00 P.M.

- **Baby must be fully awake and feeding no later than 5:00 P.M.**
- Give him a good 20 minutes on the breast he last fed on.
- **It is very important that he is not allowed the other breast until after his bath.**

5:45 P.M.

- **If baby has been very wakeful during the day or didn't nap well between 4:00 P.M. and 5:00 P.M., he may need to start his bath early.**
- Allow him to play without his diaper while preparing things needed for his bath and bedtime.

6:00 P.M.

- Baby must start his bath no later than 6:00 P.M., and be massaged and dressed by 6:15 P.M.

6:15 P.M.

- **Baby must be feeding no later than 6:15 P.M.;** this should be done in the nursery with dim lights and no talking or eye contact.
- If he did not empty the first breast at 5:00 P.M., allow 5–10 minutes before putting him on the full breast and give him a good 20–25 minutes on it.
- **It is very important that baby is in bed two hours from when he last awoke.**

7:00 P.M.

- **When he becomes drowsy settle him, fully swaddled and in the dark, with the door shut, no later than 7:00 P.M.**
- If he doesn't settle within 10–15 minutes, offer him 10 minutes from the fullest breast. Do this in the dark with no talking or eye contact.

8:00 P.M.

- **It is very important that you have a really good meal and a rest before the next feed or expressing.**

10:00–10:30 P.M.

- Turn on the lights fully and unswaddle baby so that he can wake up naturally. Allow at least ten minutes before feeding to ensure he is fully awake, so that he can feed well.
- Lay out things for the diaper change, plus a spare burp cloth sheet, and swaddle blanket in case they are needed in the middle of the night.
- Give him 20 minutes from the breast he last fed on or most of his formula, change his diaper and reswaddle him.
- **Then dim the lights and with no talking or eye contact give him 20 minutes on the second breast or the remainder of the formula. This feeding should take no longer than one hour.**

In the night

- If baby wakes before 4:00 A.M., give him a full feed.
- If he wakes between 4:00 A.M. and 5:00 A.M., give him one breast, then the second at 7:00 A.M. after expressing.
- If he wakes at 6:00 A.M., give him one breast, then the second at 7:30 A.M. after expressing.
- Make sure that you keep the lights dim and avoid eye contact or talking. Only change his diaper if absolutely necessary.

Changes to be made during the two- to four-week routine

Sleep

By three to four weeks your baby should start to show signs of being more wakeful and for longer periods. Ensure that you encourage the wakefulness during the day so that his nighttime sleep is not affected. All his sleep times, except the 4:00 P.M. one, should be in the nursery and in the dark, with the door shut. By four weeks the morning nap should be no more than one hour, to ensure that he sleeps well at lunchtime. Gradually, aim to keep him awake longer in the morning, until he is going down for his sleep at 9:00 A.M. The lunchtime nap should be no more than 2½ hours, and the afternoon nap no more than one hour in total; this nap is sometimes broken into a couple of catnaps between 4:00 P.M. and 5:00 P.M.

By four weeks he should be half swaddled (under the arms) for the 9:00 A.M. nap, and for the late afternoon nap. Around four weeks it becomes more obvious when the baby comes into his light sleep, normally every 45 minutes to one hour. If a feeding is not due, most babies, given the opportunity, settle themselves back to sleep.

Feeding

Most babies go through a growth spurt around the third week. If you are breast-feeding and have decided to give one bottle-feeding a day, this is a good age to introduce it. Introduce the bottle-feeding at 10:30 P.M., but if you wish to breast-feed for longer than six weeks, avoid giving formula at any other feedings. Consult your pediatrician if your baby is gaining less than 6 oz in weight a week.

If you decide to give a bottle-feeding at 10:30 P.M., express from both breasts at 10:00 P.M. to keep your milk supply up. This milk can be frozen and used on the occasions when you need to leave your baby with a baby-sitter.

When your baby goes through a growth spurt, reduce the amount you express at 6:45 A.M. by 1 oz and by the end of the fourth week reduce the 10:30 A.M. expressing by 1 oz. Bottle-fed babies should have their 7:00 A.M., 10:30 A.M. and 10:30 P.M. feeds increased first during growth spurts.

Development and social time

By the end of four weeks, most babies are happy to amuse themselves for short periods after they have fed. Regular social times should be well established by now. At this stage the thing your baby will love most is to listen to your voice and study your face. When he is awake, get him used to sitting in his chair for short periods; as long as he knows you are close enough, he should not become fretful. During the first four weeks when your baby is awake, get him familiar with his nursery and a few different toys. Do not overstimulate him at this age. Babies gradually uncurl during the first month, and you should encourage your baby regularly to spend 10–15 minutes under the play gym. Prop black and white or brightly colored books, especially ones with faces, around the carriage or crib when he is awake. Before the bath and in a warm room, remove his clothes and diaper. Then lay him on a changing mat on the floor, with some brightly colored toys or books to look at, so that he can have a good kick. All babies love to listen to music and to be sung to.

Routine for a breast-feeding baby at four to six weeks

Feeding times	Nap times between 7:00 A.M. and 7:00 P.M.
7:00 A.M.	9:00 A.M. to 10:00 A.M.
10:30 A.M.	11:30–12:00 noon to 2:00–2:30 P.M.
2:00–2:30 P.M.	4:15 P.M. to 5:00 P.M.
5:00 P.M.	
6:15 P.M.	
10:30 P.M.	**Maximum daily sleep 4½ hours**

EXPRESSING TIMES: 6:45 A.M., 9:45 A.M. AND 10:00 P.M.

7:00 A.M.

- **Baby should be awake, diaper changed and feeding no later than 7:00 A.M.**
- If he fed at 3:00 A.M. or 4:00 A.M., he needs 20–25 minutes on the full breast. If he's still hungry, offer 10–15 minutes from the second breast after you have expressed 2–3 oz.
- If he fed at 5:00 A.M. or 6:00 A.M., offer him 20–25 minutes from the second breast after expressing 2–3 oz.
- **Do not feed after 7:45 A.M., as it will put him off his next feed.** He can stay awake for up to two hours.

8:00 A.M.

- You should have cereal, toast and a drink no later than 8:00 A.M.

8:45 A.M.

- Baby should start to get a bit sleepy by this time. **Even if he does not show the signs, he will be getting tired, so take him to his room now.**
- Check his diaper and bedding and close the curtains.

9:00 A.M.

- **When he is drowsy, settle baby, fully or half swaddled and in the dark with the door shut, no later than 9:00 A.M.**
- He needs a sleep of no longer than one hour.
- Wash and sterilize bottles and expressing equipment.

9:45 A.M.

- Open the curtains and unswaddle baby so that he can wake up naturally.
- Prepare things for sponge bath and dressing.

10:00 A.M.

- **Baby must be fully awake now regardless of how long he slept.**
- Wash and dress him, remembering to cream all his creases and dry skin.

10:30 A.M.

- Baby should be given 20–25 minutes from the breast he last fed on.
- Lay him on his play mat so that he can move around while you express 1 oz from the second breast. Then offer him 10–15 minutes.
- **Do not feed after 11:30 A.M., as it will put him off his next feed.**

11:30 A.M.

- If baby was very alert and awake during the previous two hours, he may start to get tired by 11:30 A.M. and would need to be in bed by 11:45 A.M.

11:45 A.M.

- Regardless of what he has done earlier, he should now be taken to his room.
- Check the bedding and change his diaper.
- Close the curtains, and **when he is drowsy settle him, fully swaddled and in the dark with the door shut, no later than 12:00 noon.**

11:30–12:00 noon to 2:00–2:30 P.M.

- Baby needs a nap of no longer than 2½ hours from the time he went down.
- **If he wakes up after 45 minutes, check the swaddle, but do not talk to him or turn the lights on.**
- **Allow 20 minutes for him to resettle himself;** if he is still unsettled offer him half the 2:00 P.M. feeding.
- Try to settle him back to sleep until 2:30 P.M.

12:00 noon

- Wash and sterilize expressing equipment and then have lunch and rest before the next feeding.

2:20 P.M.

- **Baby must be awake and feeding no later than 2:30 P.M. regardless of how long he has slept.**
- Open the curtains, unswaddle him and allow him to wake up naturally. Change his diaper.
- Give 20–25 minutes from the breast he last fed on, then offer him 10–15 minutes from the other breast while you drink a large glass of water.
- **Do not feed after 3:15 P.M., as it will put him off his next feed.**
- **It is very important that he is fully awake now until 4:15 P.M., so that he goes down well at 7:00 P.M.**—if he was very alert in the morning, he may be more sleepy now. Do not put too many clothes on him, as extra warmth will make him drowsy.
- Lay him on his play mat and encourage him to play.

4:15 P.M.

- Change baby's diaper. This is a good time to take him for a walk to ensure that he sleeps well, and is refreshed for his bath and next feeding. He may start to cut right back on this nap.
- **Baby should not sleep after 5:00 P.M. if you want him to go down well at 7:00 P.M.**

5:00 P.M.

- **Baby must be fully awake, and feeding no later than 5:00 P.M.**
- Give him a good 20 minutes on the breast he last fed on.
- **It is very important that baby is not allowed the other breast until after his bath.**

5:45 P.M.

- **If he has been very wakeful during the day or did not nap well between 4:00 P.M. and 5:00 P.M., he may need to start his bath early.**
- Allow him to play without his diaper on while preparing things needed for his bath and bedtime.

6:00 P.M.

- He must start his bath no later than 6:00 P.M. and be massaged and dressed by 6:15 P.M.

6:15 P.M.

- **He must be feeding no later than 6:15 P.M.**
- **This should be done in the nursery with dim lights and no talking or eye contact.**
- If he did not empty the first breast at 5:00 P.M., allow 5–10 minutes before putting him on the full breast.
- Give him a good 20–25 minutes on the full breast while you drink a large glass of water.
- **It is very important that he is in bed two hours from when he last awoke.**

7:00 P.M.

- **Settle baby, fully or half swaddled (under the arms) and in the dark with the door shut, no later than 7:00 P.M.**

8:00 P.M.

- **It is very important for you to have a really good meal and a rest before feeding or expressing at 10:00–10:30 P.M.**

10:00–10:30 P.M.

- Turn on the lights fully and unswaddle baby so that he can wake up naturally. Allow at least ten minutes before feeding to ensure that he is fully awake, so that he can feed well.
- Lay out things for the diaper change, plus a spare sheet, burp cloth and swaddle blanket in case they are needed in the middle of the night.
- Give him 20 minutes on the first breast or most of his bottle-feeding, change his diaper and reswaddle him.
- **Dim the lights, and with no talking or eye contact give him 20 minutes on the second breast or the remainder of the bottle-feeding.**
- **This feeding should take no longer than one hour.**

In the night

- If he wakes up before 4:00 A.M., give him a full feeding.
- If he wakes up between 4:00 A.M. and 5:00 A.M. give one breast, then the second at 7:00 A.M. after expressing.
- If he wakes up at 6:00 A.M., give one breast, then the second at 7:30 A.M. after expressing.
- Always avoid eye contact and talking, and keep the lights low. Don't change his diaper unless absolutely necessary.

Changes to be made during the four- to six-week routine

Sleep

Your baby should start to sleep a longer stretch in the night around now. Once he has done this stretch several nights in a row, try not to feed him if he suddenly goes back to waking up earlier again. Try settling him with some water or a cuddle.

His total daily nap time between 7:00 A.M. and 7:30 P.M. should be reduced to a strict 4½ hours: the morning nap should be no more than one hour, the lunchtime nap no more than 2½ hours and the afternoon nap no more than 30 minutes between 4:15 and 5:00 P.M. By the end of six weeks, he should be half swaddled (under the arms) at the 9:00 A.M. and the 4:15 P.M. naps.

It should now take less time to settle your baby to sleep; watch that he is not getting used to falling asleep on the breast or with a pacifier. Now is the time to get him used to going down when he is more awake. Often a lullaby light, which plays a tune and casts images on the ceiling for ten minutes or so, will help a baby to settle himself.

Feeding

If he starts to wake up earlier in the night, try settling him with water and a cuddle. If you find you have to wake him at 7:00 A.M. every morning, very gradually and by a small amount, cut back the amount of milk he is taking in the night. This will cause him to drink more during the day and less in the night, and eventually he will drop the middle-of-the-night feeding altogether.

Increase the day feedings, not the night feedings. Cut back on the first expressing of the day by a further 1 oz, and by the end of six weeks cut out the 10:30 A.M. expressing completely. Most babies are happy to wait longer after the 7:00 A.M. feeding, so gradually keep pushing the 10:00 A.M. feeding forward until your baby is feeding at 10:30 A.M.

Most babies go through a second growth spurt at six weeks, and want to spend longer on the breast at some feedings. Bottle-fed babies should have the 7:00 A.M., the 10:30 A.M. and then the 6:15 P.M. feedings increased first during growth spurts.

Development and social time

Most babies are much more alert at this age, and will enjoy focusing for longer periods on posters, cards and a colorful room border. Buy a selection of these and stick them to cardboard so that they can be moved to different places. Your baby should be showing more interest in his toys now, and should be happy to kick under his play gym or mobile for 20–30 minutes. Try to take him to a baby massage class once a week. He should have more head control now, so encourage him to practice push-ups when he is lying on his tummy on the changing mat, but **never leave him alone on the changing mat.**

Start to show him simple baby books for 5–10 minutes each day and point to and name the different images. Sing nursery rhymes with lots of *s*'s in them; the shape your mouth makes when singing these songs will encourage him to smile. He will be making gurgling and cooing noises and will enjoy your imitating any new noises he may make.

Routine for a breast-feeding baby at six to eight weeks

Feeding times	Nap times between 7:00 A.M. and 7:00 P.M.
7:00 A.M.	9:00 A.M.–9:45 A.M.
10:45 A.M.	11:45/12:00 noon–2:00/2:30 P.M.
2:00/2:30 P.M.	4:30 P.M.–5:00 P.M.
6:15 P.M.	
10:30 P.M.	**Maximum daily sleep 4 hours**

EXPRESSING TIMES: 6:45 A.M. AND 10:00 P.M.

7:00 A.M.

- **Baby should be awake, diaper changed and feeding no later than 7:00 A.M.**
- If he fed at 4:00 A.M. or 5:00 A.M., offer him 20–25 minutes on the full breast. If he's still hungry, offer 10–15 minutes from the second breast after you have expressed 1–2 oz.
- If he fed at 6:00 A.M., offer him 20–25 minutes from the second breast after you have expressed 1–2 oz.
- **Do not feed after 7:45 A.M., as it will put him off his next feeding.** He can stay awake for up to two hours.

8:00 A.M.

- You should have cereal, toast and a drink no later than 8:00 A.M.
- Wash and dress baby, remembering to cream all his creases and dry skin.

8:50 A.M.

- Check his diaper and bedding and close the curtains.

9:00 A.M.

- **Settle the drowsy baby, half swaddled and in the dark with the door shut, no later than 9:00 A.M.**
- He needs a sleep of no longer than 45 minutes.
- Wash and sterilize bottles and expressing equipment.

9:45 A.M.

- Open the curtains and unswaddle baby so that he can wake up naturally.

10:00 A.M.

- **Baby must be fully awake now regardless of how long he slept.**
- If he had a full feed at 7:00 A.M., he should last until 10:45 A.M. for his next feed. If he fed earlier followed by a little extra at 7:30 A.M., he may need to start this feed slightly earlier.
- Encourage him to play under his play gym.

10:45 A.M.

- He should be given 20–25 minutes from the breast he last fed on, then offered 10–15 minutes from the second breast while you have a large glass of water.
- **Do not feed after 11:30 A.M., as it will put him off his next feeding.**

11:45 A.M.

- Regardless of what he has done earlier, he should now be taken to his room.
- Check the bedding and change his diaper.
- Close the curtains and **settle baby, half or fully swaddled and in the dark with the door shut, no later than 12:00 noon.**

11:45–12:00 noon to 2:00–2:30 P.M.

- Baby needs a nap of no longer than 2½ hours from the time he went down.

12:00 noon

- Wash and sterilize bottles and expressing equipment, then have lunch and a rest before the next feeding.

2:30 P.M.

- **Baby must be awake and feeding no later than 2:30 P.M. regardless of how long he has slept.**
- Open the curtains, unswaddle him and allow him to wake up naturally. Change his diaper.
- Give 20–25 minutes from the breast he last fed on, then offer him 10–15 minutes from the other breast while you drink a large glass of water.
- **Do not feed after 3:15 P.M., as it will put him off his next feed.**
- **It is very important that he is fully awake now until 4:30 P.M., so that he goes down well at 7:00 A.M.**
- If he was very alert in the morning, he may be more sleepy now. Do not put too many clothes on him, as extra warmth will make him drowsy.
- Lay him on his play mat and encourage him to kick.

4:15 P.M.

- Change his diaper and offer him a drink of cooled boiled water or well-diluted juice no later than 4:30 P.M.
- This is a good time to take him for a walk to ensure that he sleeps well, and is refreshed for his bath and next feeding.

5:00 P.M.

- **Baby must be fully awake now if you want him to go down well at 7:00 P.M.**
- If he is very hungry, offer him 10–15 minutes on the breast he last fed on, otherwise try and get him to wait until after his bath for a full feeding. By eight weeks he should be happy to wait until after the bath.

5:30 P.M.

- Allow him to play without his diaper while preparing things needed for his bath and bedtime.

5:45 P.M.

- He must start his bath no later than 5:45 P.M., and be massaged and dressed by 6:15 P.M.

6:15 P.M.

- **He must be feeding no later than 6:15 P.M., and this should be done in the nursery with dim lights and no talking or eye contact.**
- If he fed at 5:00 P.M., allow him a further 10–15 minutes to empty that breast completely, before putting him on the second breast.
- If he did not feed at 5:00 P.M., he should start on the breast he last fed on. Give him 20 minutes on each breast while you drink a large glass of water.
- **It is very important that he is in bed two hours from when he last woke up.**

7:00 P.M.

- **Settle baby, half swaddled and in the dark with the door shut, no later than 7:00 P.M.**

8:00 P.M.

- **It is very important that you have a really good meal and a rest before the next feeding or expressing.**

10:00–10:30 P.M.

- Turn on the lights fully and unswaddle baby so that he can wake up naturally. Allow at least ten minutes before feeding to ensure that he is fully awake, so that he can feed well.
- Lay out things for the diaper change, plus a spare diaper sheet, burp cloth and swaddle blanket in case they are needed in the middle of the night.
- Give him 20 minutes on the first breast or most of his bottle, change his diaper and reswaddle him.

- **Dim the lights and with no talking or eye contact give him 20 minutes on the second breast or the remainder of the bottle.**
- **This feeding should take no longer than one hour.**

In the night

- If he is feeding before 4:00 A.M., feeding well and losing interest in his 7:00 A.M. feed, it would be wise to try settling him with some cool boiled water. If he even takes an ounce or two before going on the breast, it should cause him to feed better at 7:00 A.M. The aim is to get him to take all his daily requirements between 7:00 A.M. and 11:00 P.M. If he is gaining 6–8 oz of weight each week, it is important that he is encouraged to cut down and eventually drop the night feed.
- If he wakes between 4:00 A.M. and 5:00 A.M. give one breast, then the second at 7:00 A.M. after expressing.
- If he wakes up at 6:00 A.M. give one breast, then the second at 7:30 A.M. after expressing.
- As before, keep lights low and any stimulation to a minimum. No diaper change unless absolutely necessary.

Changes to be made during the six- to eight-week routine

Sleep

Most babies should be sleeping longer in the night now. Once he has lasted longer for several nights in a row, try not to feed your baby before that time again.

Cut back his daily nap time by 30 minutes, to a daily total of four hours. The morning nap should be no more than 45 minutes, the lunchtime nap should be between 2¼ and 2½ hours, no longer, and the afternoon nap should be no more than 30 minutes. He may catnap on and off during this nap; some babies cut out this nap altogether. Do not allow him to cut out this nap if he is not managing to stay awake until 7:00 P.M. If you want him to sleep till 7:00 A.M., it is important that he goes to sleep nearer 7:00 P.M.

He should now be half swaddled at the 9:00 A.M. and 7:00 P.M. naps, and at 12:00 noon by the end of eight weeks. Once he has slept through the night for two weeks, he can be half swaddled throughout the night. He should be sleeping some of the time in his big crib, gradually preparing him for sleeping there throughout the night.

Feeding

If your baby suddenly goes back to waking up earlier again, wait ten minutes or so before going to him. If he will not settle himself back to sleep, try settling him with some water or a cuddle.

Keep increasing day feedings, not night feedings. Most babies are happy to wait longer after the 7:00 A.M. feed, so keep pushing this feed forward until he is feeding at 10:45 A.M. Cut back on the first expressing of the day by a further 1 oz, and by the end of eight weeks cut out the 6:45 A.M. expressing altogether. By the end of eight weeks he should have dropped the 5:00 P.M. feeding, and be having a small drink of cool boiled water. Once the 5:00 P.M. feed is dropped, the time of the bath should be brought forward to allow the baby enough time to take both breasts or a full bottle.

Most babies go through a second growth spurt at six weeks and want to spend longer on the breast at some feedings. Bottle-fed babies should have the 7:00 A.M., 10:45 A.M. and 6:15 P.M. feedings increased first during growth spurts. The 10:30 P.M. feeding should only be increased if all the other feedings have been increased, and he is not going a longer spell in the night. Try not to give more than 6 oz at this feeding.

Development and social time

Your baby should be very alert at all his wakeful times now. If he is properly awake for eight hours between 7:00 A.M. and 7:00 P.M., it will also encourage him to sleep for longer in the night.

You should spend a short time every day doing baby exercises—there are books available to show how these are done. Encourage longer spells on his tummy on the floor, also rolling and reaching for toys. Give him small soft rattles to hold. He will follow you with his eyes when you move around the room, and will respond to your voice with lots of smiles and gurgling. Continue to show him different baby books and play lots of different types of music.

Routine for a breast-feeding baby
at eight to twelve weeks

Feeding times	Nap times between 7:00 A.M. and 7:00 P.M.
7:00 A.M.	9:00 A.M.–9:45 A.M.
10:45/11:00 A.M.	12:00 noon to 2:00/2:15 P.M.
2:00/2:15 P.M.	4:45 P.M.–5:00 P.M.
6:15 P.M.	
10:30 P.M.	**Maximum daily sleep 3½ hours**

EXPRESSING AT 10:00 P.M.

7:00 A.M.

- **Baby should be awake, diaper changed and feeding no later than 7:00 A.M.**
- He should be given 20 minutes from the first breast, then offered 10–15 minutes from the second breast.
- **Do not feed after 7:45 A.M., as it will put him off his next feeding.**
- He can stay awake for up to two hours.

8:00 A.M.

- You should have cereal, toast and a drink no later than 8:00 A.M.
- Wash and dress baby, remembering to cream all his creases and dry skin.

8:50 A.M.

- Check his diaper and bedding and close the curtains.

9:00 A.M.

- **Settle the drowsy baby, half swaddled and in the dark with the door shut, no later than 9:00 A.M.**
- He needs a sleep of no longer than 45 minutes.
- Wash and sterilize bottles and expressing equipment.

9:45 A.M.

- Open the curtains and unswaddle baby so that he can wake up naturally.

10:00 A.M.

- Baby must be fully awake now regardless of how long he slept.
- Encourage him to kick under his play gym.

10:45–11:00 A.M.

- He should be given 20 minutes from the breast he last fed on, then offered 10–15 minutes from the second breast while you have a large glass of water.
- **Do not feed after 11:30 A.M., as it will put him off his next feed.**

11:55 A.M.

- Regardless of what he has done earlier he should now be taken to his room.
- Check the sheet and change his diaper.
- Close the curtains and **settle baby, half swaddled and in the dark with the door shut, no later than 12:00 noon.**

12:00 noon to 2:00–2:15 P.M.

- Baby needs a nap of no longer than 2¼ hours from the time he went down.
- Wash and sterilize bottles and expressing equipment.

2:00–2:15 P.M.

- **Baby must be awake 2¼ hours from the time he went down, regardless of how he has slept, and he must be feeding no later than 2:30 P.M.**
- Open the curtains, unswaddle him and allow him to wake up naturally. Change his diaper.

- Give 20 minutes from the breast he last fed on, then offer him 10–15 minutes from the other breast while you drink a large glass of water.
- **Do not feed after 3:15 P.M., as it will put him off his next feeding.**
- **It is very important that he is fully awake now until 4:45 P.M. so that he goes down well at 7:00 P.M.**

4:15 P.M.

- Change his diaper, and offer him a drink of cooled boiled water no later than 4:30 P.M.
- He may have a short nap between 4:45 P.M. and 5:00 P.M.

5:00 P.M.

- **Baby must be fully awake if you want him to sleep at 7:00 P.M.**
- He should be happy to wait until after the bath for his feeding.

5:30 P.M.

- Allow him to play without his diaper while preparing things needed for his bath and bedtime.

5:45 P.M.

- He must start his bath no later than 5:45 P.M., and be massaged and dressed by 6:15 P.M.

6:15 P.M.

- **He must be feeding no later than 6:15 P.M., and this should be done in the nursery with dim lights and no talking or eye contact.**
- He should be given 20 minutes on each breast while you drink a large glass of water.
- **It is very important that he is in bed two hours from when he last awoke.**

7:00 P.M.

- **Settle the drowsy baby, half swaddled and in the dark with the door shut, no later than 7:00 P.M.**

8:00 P.M.

- **It is very important that you have a really good meal and a rest before the next feeding or expressing.**

10:00–10:30 P.M.

- Turn on the lights fully and unswaddle baby so that he can wake up naturally. Allow at least ten minutes before feeding to ensure that he is fully awake, so that he can feed well.
- Lay out things for the diaper change, plus a spare sheet, burp cloth and swaddle blanket in case they are needed in the middle of the night.
- Give him 20 minutes on the first breast or most of his bottle, change his diaper and reswaddle him.
- **Dim the lights and with no talking or eye contact give him 20 minutes on the second breast or the remainder of the bottle.**
- **This feeding should take no longer than one hour.**

In the night

- If your baby is feeding before 5:00 A.M., feeding well and losing interest in his 7:00 A.M. feed, it would be wise to try settling him with some cool boiled water. Remember, the aim is to get him to take all his daily requirements between 7:00 A.M. and 11:00 P.M. As long as he is gaining 6 oz a week, he can be encouraged to go through to 5:00 A.M. without a milk feed.
- If he wakes up at 5:00 A.M. give him the first breast, and if needed five to ten minutes on the second breast.
- If he wakes up at 6:00 A.M. give the first breast, then the second at 7:30 A.M.
- Avoid nighttime stimulation; only change his diaper if necessary.

Changes to be made during the eight- to twelve-week routine

Sleep

Most babies should be going through the night at this age, although a totally breast-fed baby may still be waking up once in the night, hopefully nearer 5:00 A.M. or 6:00 A.M.

Cut back your baby's daily nap time by a further 30 minutes, to a daily total of three hours. The morning nap should be no more than 45 minutes, but if he is not sleeping so well at lunchtime, it can be cut back to 30 minutes. The lunchtime nap should be no more than 2¼ hours. Most babies have cut out their late afternoon nap, but if not do not allow more than 15 minutes. All babies should only be half swaddled and sleeping in their big cribs; particular attention should be paid when tucking the baby in the crib. One reason many babies of this age still wake up is because they move around the crib and get their arms and legs caught in between the bars. (See pages 3–5 for further details on cribs and bedding.)

Feeding

Keep pushing the 10:45 A.M. feed forward until he is feeding at 11:00 A.M. If he is sleeping regularly to 7:00 A.M., gradually bring the 10:30–11:00 P.M. feed forward, by five minutes every three nights until he is feeding at 10:00 P.M. He should be well established on five feeds a day now, eventually taking a very small feed at 10:00 P.M. If he is totally breast-fed and has started waking up earlier in the morning, it may be worth trying to give a small bottle of either expressed or formula milk after you feed him at 10:00 P.M.

If you are considering introducing a further bottle-feeding, the best time to introduce it is at the 11:00 A.M. feeding. Gradually reduce the time of the feed by two to three minutes each day and add a small amount of formula. By the end of the first week, if your baby is taking a bottle of 5–6 oz, you should be able to drop the breast-feed easily without the risk of serious engorgement. Increase the bottle-feed to suit your baby's needs. Bottle-fed babies should continue to have their 7:00 A.M., 11:00 A.M. and 6:15 P.M. feeds increased first during growth spurts. Unless you have a very hungry baby, the 2:30 P.M. feeding should be 1 oz less than the other feedings so that he feeds well at 6:15 P.M.

Development and social time

Your baby should be able to stay awake easily when out in the stroller, and will enjoy sitting slightly elevated so that he can look around. Enroll him in a baby swimming class. He will spend a lot of time looking at his hands and chewing them. Encourage him to reach for toys and hold them and to roll from back to front.

Routine for a baby
at three to four months

Feeding times	Nap times between 7:00 A.M. and 7:00 P.M.
7:00 A.M.	9:00 A.M. to 9:45 A.M.
11:00 A.M.	12:00 noon to 2:00–2:15 P.M.
2:15–2:30 P.M.	
6:15 P.M.	
10:30 P.M.	MAXIMUM DAILY SLEEP 3 HOURS

7:00 A.M.

- **Baby should be awake, diaper changed and feeding no later than 7:00 A.M.**
- He should feed from both breasts or a full bottle and then should stay awake for two hours.

8:00 A.M.

- He should be encouraged to kick on his play mat for 20–30 minutes.
- Wash and dress baby, remembering to cream all his creases and dry skin.

9:00 A.M.

- **Settle the drowsy baby, half swaddled and in the dark with the door shut no later than 9:00 A.M.** He needs a sleep of no longer than 45 minutes.
- Wash and sterilize bottles and expressing equipment.

9:45 A.M.

- Open the curtains and unswaddle him so that he can wake up naturally.

10:00 A.M.

- **Baby must be fully awake now regardless of how long he slept.**
- Encourage him to play under his play gym.

11:00 A.M.

- He should be given a feeding from both breasts or a full bottle.
- Do not feed after 11:30 A.M., as it will put him off his next feeding.

11:50 A.M.

- Check the sheet and change his diaper.
- Close the curtains and **settle the drowsy baby, half swaddled and in the dark with the door shut, no later than 12:00 noon.**

12:00 noon to 2:00–2:15 P.M.

- Baby needs a nap of no longer than 2¼ hours from the time he went down. Wash and sterilize bottles and expressing equipment.

2:00–2:15 P.M.

- **Baby must be awake 2¼ hours from the time he was put to bed, regardless of how long he has slept, and he must be feeding no later than 2:30 P.M.**
- Open the curtains, unswaddle him and allow him to wake naturally, then change his diaper.
- He needs a feeding from both breasts or a bottle.
- **Do not feed him after 3:15 P.M., as it will put him off his next feeding.**
- If he has slept well at both naps, he should manage to get through the rest of the afternoon without another nap.

4:15 P.M.

- Change his diaper and offer him a drink of cool boiled water no later than 4:30 P.M.

5:30 P.M.

- Put him on the changing mat on the floor without his diaper, so that he can play while you prepare his bath.

5:45 P.M.

- Baby must start his bath no later than 5:45 P.M., and be massaged and dressed no later than 6:15 P.M.

6:15 P.M.

- **He must be feeding no later than 6:15 P.M.**
- He should feed from both breasts or have 7–8 oz of formula.
- Dim the lights and sit him in his chair for ten minutes while you tidy up.

7:00 P.M.

- **Settle the drowsy baby, half swaddled and in the dark with the door shut, no later than 7:00 P.M.**

10:30 P.M.

- Turn the lights on low and wake him enough to feed.
- Give him most of his breast-feed or a 6-oz bottle, change his diaper and half swaddle him.
- **Dim the lights and with no talking or eye contact give him the remainder of his feed. If he does not want the remainder do not force it, as he should start to cut back on this feed now.**
- This feed should take no longer than 30 minutes.

Changes to be made during the three- to four-month routine

Sleep

Your baby will cut right back on his late afternoon sleep. Some days he may manage to get through the afternoon without the nap, but may need to go to bed five to ten minutes earlier. The time your baby is awake at the 10:30 P.M. feed should be gradually reduced to 30 minutes.

Feeding

If your baby continues to sleep through to 7:00 A.M. once his waking time at 10:30 P.M. has been reduced to 30 minutes, start reducing the amount he is drinking at 10:00–10:30 P.M. Only continue with this if he is sleeping well until 7:00 A.M. Once he is taking 2 oz at the last feed and sleeps through to 7:00 A.M. consecutively for seven nights, drop this feed.

Development and social time

He should spend most of his social time on the floor kicking and rolling, reaching for toys and holding them for short spells. Encourage lots of grabbing and holding. He should go on his tummy for a short spell every day. He should go swimming once a week and have one other social activity. Read to your baby every day and also make sure he listens to a wide variety of music. Encourage him to help hold his bottle but never allow him to feed by himself or prop the bottle up.

Robert: aged four months

Robert was being totally breast-fed apart from one feed of formula when his mother contacted me. She was very concerned that despite introducing solids he still was demanding to be fed every two hours, day and night. He seemed to have none of the usual association problems, and he would, when ready to sleep, go down in his crib happily without needing to be rocked, patted or fed.

When he did wake in the night, he would feed quickly and go straight back to sleep. The only real problem was that he needed to be fed every two hours.

He went from a weight of just over 8 lb at birth to 16 lb at four months. This was an excellent weight gain, and certainly proved he was getting enough to eat. I suggested that his mother should continue to give Robert the baby rice, but introduce it after the 6:00 P.M. feed instead of the 2:30 P.M. one. The one bottle feed should be moved to 10:30 P.M., instead of 10:30 A.M. For the rest of his milk feeds and his sleep, I advised her to put him on the six-week routine. If he adapted to that routine well, she should gradually move him through the routines until he was on the one suitable for his age.

By the end of two weeks, Robert was happily established in the four-month routine, and sleeping through most nights from the 10:30 P.M. feed to 7:00 A.M. Unfortunately Robert's parents had only enjoyed a week of him sleeping through regularly to 7:00 A.M. when he developed a cold. He continued to feed well, his routine during the day was fine and he also settled well at 7:00 P.M., but like most young babies who develop a cold he became very unsettled in the middle of the night. His parents propped up his crib and used a vaporizer, but the mucus in Robert's nose caused him so much distress that the only way his mother could keep him calm was to put him upright on her chest. The cold lingered on for nearly two weeks, and by the time he was completely clear of the cold he was so used to waking up at 3:00 A.M. that he continued to do so. The mother was exhausted by this time, and so ended up giving him a pacifier at the 3:00 A.M. waking. As I predicted, he started to look for it during other sleeps.

By the time he reached six months, all his naps had gone wrong. He was difficult to settle at 7:00 P.M. and would wake up regularly in the night. I suggested sleep training, but the mother felt sure he would eventually break the pattern. At the end of seven months, she decided to take the pacifier away completely, as things were so out of hand, and within a couple of nights of leaving him to cry for 20–30 minutes he had learned to settle himself. He did continue to wake up at least once in the middle of the night, but the parents usually got him back to sleep by stroking his forehead.

The mother was returning to work when Robert was nine months old, and she realized that with her demanding job she would not be able to cope if he continued to wake up even once a night. The parents by this time had spoken to several other couples who had done sleep training, and decided it was now or never. Sadly for them and the baby, they did not adhere to the golden rule when sleep training a baby, which is never to pick the baby up when he is crying. They would let him cry for 30 to 50 minutes, and become so overwhelmed with guilt that they would then pick him up and rock him to sleep even though I had told them repeatedly that sleep training should only be done if the parents feel they are disciplined enough to carry it through. By picking the baby up after 40 minutes of crying, they were actually teaching him that if he cried long enough he would get picked up. Even worse, because he was so exhausted from being awake in the night, he became very unhappy and irritable during the daytime.

The mother, now back at work, became so exhausted trying to cope with work and getting up in the night that she decided to give sleep training one last try. I put her in contact with several mothers who had gone through a similar situation, in the hope that this would give her confidence to follow the sleep training properly. The first night Robert cried for over three hours; the parents did not go in at all. They lay in bed holding hands and crying themselves, and vowing never to let it get to this stage if they had a second baby. The second night he cried again for three hours; but this time there were longer intervals between the crying. On the third night he slept through from 7:30 P.M. to 7:00 A.M., and continued to sleep well for many months until he caught another cold. This time when he was over the cold, they immediately left him to settle himself, which only took a couple of nights of very little crying.

   The majority of babies will automatically go back into the routine the minute they recover from an illness, but a few, like Robert, do have to be sleep trained.

Routine for a baby
at four to five months

Feeding times	Nap times between 7:00 A.M. and 7:00 P.M.
7:00 A.M.	9:00 A.M. to 9:45 A.M.
11:00 A.M.	12:00 noon to 2:00–2:15 P.M.
2:30 P.M.	
6:00 P.M.	
10:00 P.M.	**MAXIMUM DAILY SLEEP 3 HOURS**

7:00 A.M.

- **Baby should be awake, diaper changed and feeding no later than 7:00 A.M.**
- He should feed from both breasts or have a full bottle.
- He should stay awake for two hours.

8:00 A.M.

- He should be encouraged to play on his play mat for 20–30 minutes.
- Wash and dress baby, remembering to cream all his creases and dry skin.

9:00 A.M.

- **Settle the drowsy baby, half swaddled and in the dark with the door shut no later than 9:00 A.M.** He needs a sleep of no longer than 45 minutes.
- Wash and sterilize bottles and expressing equipment.

9:45 A.M.

- Open the curtains and unswaddle him so that he can wake up naturally.

10:00 A.M.

- **Baby must be fully awake now regardless of how long he slept.** Encourage him to kick under his play gym or take him on an outing.

11:00 A.M.

- He should be given a full breast-feed or a full bottle-feed before being offered a small amount of rice cereal.
- Encourage him to sit in his chair while you clear away the lunch things.

11:50 A.M.

- Check the sheet and change his diaper.
- Close the curtains and **settle the drowsy baby, half swaddled in the dark with the door shut no later than 12:00 noon.**

12:00 noon to 2:00–2:15 P.M.

- **He will need a nap now of no longer than 2¼ hours from the time he went down.** Wash and sterilize bottles and expressing equipment.

2:15 P.M./2:30 P.M.

- **Baby must be awake 2¼ hours from the time he went down, regardless of how long he has slept, and he must be feeding no later than 2:30 P.M.**
- Open the curtains, unswaddle him and allow him to wake up naturally. Change his diaper.
- He needs a feed from both breasts or a full bottle.
- **Do not feed him after 3:15 P.M. as it will put him off his next feed.**
- If he has slept well at both naps, he may manage to get through the rest of the afternoon without a further sleep.

4:15 P.M.

- Change baby's diaper, and offer him a drink of cool boiled water no later than 4:30 P.M.

5:15 P.M.

- Put him on the changing mat on the floor without his diaper so that he can kick while you prepare the bath.

5:30 P.M.

- He must start his bath no later than 5:35 P.M., and be massaged and dressed no later than 6:00 P.M.

6:00 P.M.

- **He must be feeding no later than 6:00 P.M.**
- He should feed from both breasts or have a full bottle, before having the rice and cereal.
- Then dim the lights and sit him in his chair for ten minutes while you tidy up.

7:00 P.M.

- **Settle the drowsy baby, half swaddled and in the dark with the door shut, no later than 7:00 P.M.**

10:00 P.M.

- Turn the lights on low and wake him enough to feed.
- Give him most of his breast or bottle feed, change his diaper and half swaddle him.
- **Dim the lights, and with no talking or eye contact give him the remainder of the feed. If he does not want the remainder do not force it, as he should start to cut back on this feed now.**
- **This feed should take no longer than 30 minutes.**

Changes to be made during the four- to five-month routine

Sleep

By the end of five months, your baby should be sleeping from 7:00 P.M. to 7:00 A.M. If he is not sleeping the full two hours at lunchtime, cut back on his morning nap.

Feeding

If solids are introduced at four months, it is important that your baby still has most of his milk feed first. Bath time should be brought forward to allow enough time to give the rice cereal and fruit purée after the milk. Once solids are introduced at 6:00 P.M., if he has not already dropped the 10:30 P.M. feed, it should be brought forward to 10:00 P.M. and then dropped by five months. He should be enjoying a varied selection of vegetables and fruit from the first stage weaning foods (see page 146).

Development and social time

Your baby should spend most of his social time on the floor kicking and rolling, reaching for toys and holding them for short spells. Encourage lots of grabbing and holding and encourage him to help hold his bottle. He should still go on his tummy for a short spell every day and also should be read to every day and listen to a wide variety of music.

He should go swimming once a week and have one other social activity.

Routine for a baby
at five to six months

Feeding times	Nap times between 7:00 A.M. and 7:00 P.M.
7:00 A.M.	9:00 A.M. to 9:45 A.M.
11:30 A.M.	12:15 P.M. to 2:00–2:15 P.M.
2:30 P.M.	
6:00 P.M.	**MAXIMUM DAILY SLEEP 3 HOURS**

7:00 A.M.

- **Baby should be awake, diaper changed and feeding no later than 7:00 A.M.**
- He should feed from both breasts or have a full bottle, followed by a small amount of breakfast cereal mixed with either expressed milk or formula.
- He should stay awake for two hours.

8:00 A.M.

- He should be encouraged to kick on his play mat for 20–30 minutes.
- Wash and dress baby, remembering to cream all his creases and dry skin.

9:00 A.M.

- **Settle the drowsy baby, half swaddled and in the dark with the door shut, no later than 9:00 A.M.**
- He needs a sleep of no longer than 45 minutes.

9:45 A.M.

- Open the curtains and unswaddle him so that he can wake up naturally.

10:00 A.M.

- **Baby must be fully awake now regardless of how long he slept.**
- Encourage him to play under his play gym or take him on an outing.

11:30 A.M.

- He should be given half the milk feed followed by a selection of puréed vegetables, then offered the rest of the milk feed.
- Encourage him to sit in his chair while you clear away the lunch things.

12:10 P.M.

- Check the sheet and change his diaper.
- **Close the curtains and settle the drowsy baby, half swaddled and in the dark with the door shut, no later than 12:15 P.M.**

12:15 P.M. to 2:00–2:15 P.M.

- **He will need a nap now of no longer than two hours from the time he went down.**
- Wash and sterilize bottles and expressing equipment.

2:15 P.M.

- **Baby must be awake and feeding no later than 2:30 P.M. regardless of how long he has slept.**
- Open the curtains, unswaddle him and allow him to wake up naturally. Change his diaper.
- He needs a feed from both breasts or a full bottle-feed.
- **Do not feed him after 3:15 P.M., as it will put him off his next feed.**

4:15 P.M.

- Change baby's diaper, and offer him a drink of cool boiled water no later than 4:30 P.M.

5:15 P.M.

- Put him on the changing mat on the floor without his diaper, so he can play while you prepare the bath.

5:30 P.M.

- He must start his bath no later than 5:30 P.M., and be massaged and dressed no later than 6:00 P.M.

6:00 P.M.

- **Baby must be feeding no later than 6:00 P.M.**
- He should feed from both breasts or have a full bottle before having the rice cereal and fruit.
- Dim the lights and sit him in his chair for ten minutes while you tidy up.

7:00 P.M.

- **Baby should be half swaddled and settled in the dark with the door shut no later than 7:00 P.M.**

Changes to be made during the five- to six-month routine

Sleep

Your baby should continue to sleep well between 7:00 P.M. and 7:00 A.M. The lunchtime nap should be pushed to 12:15 P.M. to fit in with the later lunch. If he is not sleeping the full two hours at lunchtime, cut back on his morning nap.

Feeding

Once solids are established at 11:30 A.M. and 6:00 P.M., introduce cereal after the 7:00 A.M. milk feed, and continue to give all the milk feed first at breakfast. When solids are established at breakfast, the time of lunch should gradually be pushed to 11:30 A.M. The tier system of feeding should be used now: this is when you alternate between milk and solids during a feed. By the end of six months, he should be taking more solids than milk at 11:30 A.M. Once he is taking more solids at 11:30 A.M., he may need to increase the 2:30 P.M. milk feed.

Development and social time

Your baby should spend more time on his tummy to encourage crawling. He may enjoy going in a bouncer that hangs from a door frame and may be able to sit up unaided for short spells surrounded by cushions. He will grab hold of and play with small soft rattles for short periods.

James: aged 5½ months

James was 5½ months when his mother first called me, as his parents were mentally and physically exhausted. James was settling well at 7:00 P.M., but woke up several times a night, sometimes staying awake for two hours at a time. No amount of feeding, rocking or walking the floor would pacify him. He was drinking well in excess of 48 oz of formula a day, refusing solids, and never slept a wink between 7:00 A.M. and 7:00 P.M.

This was a particularly unusual case for me to try and solve. Normally I find that one of the main causes of repeated night wakings with babies over three months of age is that they are having too much sleep between 7:00 A.M. and 7:00 P.M. This was not the case with James, and what a challenge he turned out to be! I observed him for the first 24 hours before deciding what plan of action to take. Unbelievably, he did not shut his eyes the whole day, and even more surprisingly he did not get hysterically overtired like babies of his age would normally if they have gone long spells without sleep. However, he did need constant attention and entertainment, which was absolutely exhausting for the poor mother, who had also been awake most of the night.

James would drink an 8-oz bottle of formula, but go berserk every time he was offered a spoonful of solids. I suggested that at 6:00 P.M. we should try giving him only half of the formula, then offer the solids, but the same thing happened: he went berserk again. He would not stop screaming until we allowed him to finish the full 8 oz of formula. We then proceeded to bathe and settle him for the night, and he went to sleep like a dream at 7:00 P.M. just as his mother said he would. At 10:30 P.M. I woke him up for his last feed, when he drank 7 oz quickly, burped well and settled quickly back to sleep.

That night the parents each took a sleeping pill plus a glass of red wine, and moved up to the top floor to get some much needed sleep.

With James "sleeping like a baby" in the room next to mine, I was fast coming to the conclusion that the only real problem with James was that he was a milk-aholic and had very neurotic parents. I was convinced that with my expert handling, the problem of nighttime waking would be quickly solved! At 1:00 A.M. the screaming started, but refusing to believe that he could be hungry, I tried to settle him with a cuddle and some cool boiled water. It took me nearly 40 minutes to get him back to sleep, only to be awoken by the most horrendous screaming an hour and a half later. This time he would not be pacified with water and a cuddle but kicked and screamed so much I thought he was going to go into a fit. All my logic went out the window; I thought it must be hunger and offered him a full 8-oz bottle, which he quickly drank. I changed his diaper and settled him back in his crib, where he gurgled and talked to himself for another 30 minutes before going to sleep at 4:00 A.M. He awoke again at 5:00 A.M., one hour later. I now decided to get tough and use the controlled crying method. I went in every ten minutes to reassure him, but it was an hour and ten minutes before he eventually fell asleep at 6:10 A.M. He then awoke on the dot of 7:00 A.M. in the happiest of moods, despite having been awake for nearly three hours in the night. The thought of trying to keep him entertained during the 12-hour day ahead, with no sleep for either him or me, filled me with horror. I very quickly decided the parents were not neurotic, but saints for having coped with him this far.

That day I decided that although he showed no signs of ever wanting to sleep during the day, I would try my routine for a five to six-month baby. I put him down in the morning at 9:00 A.M., and he screamed for 25 minutes before dropping off to sleep. I then had to wake him at 10:00 A.M. I put him back down at 12:00 noon, and again he screamed for nearly 25 minutes, going to sleep at 12:25 P.M. and waking up screaming 45 minutes later when he came into his light sleep. He screamed on and off for a further 45 minutes before falling asleep at 2:00 P.M. Although it was very tempting to let him sleep past 2:30 P.M., I knew from past experience how important it was not to let a baby sleep past the feeding time, as the structuring of feeds in the early months plays a very important part in babies' sleep cycles. He stayed awake until 4:45 P.M., at which time he had a 15-minute nap in the carriage while out for a walk. We followed the same bath time ritual, and he went down well at 7:00 P.M., and like the previous night I fed him at 11:00 P.M., after which he settled well and went straight back to sleep.

He woke around 1:00 A.M., and I decided to keep going with the con-

trolled crying method, as the first waking in the night was due to habit more than hunger. I went in every 15–20 minutes to reassure him, and again like the previous night it took about 45 minutes to settle him.

He then woke up again at 3:00 A.M., and this time it took around 30 minutes to settle him. When he woke for the third time at 5:00 A.M., I felt that having gone over six hours for the first time ever without a feed he might be hungry, so I fed him. He took 7 oz quickly, but did not settle until 6:15 A.M., and then woke up on the dot of 7:00 A.M. The days and nights that followed formed much the same pattern for a further week, showing no real sign of improvement. I was beginning to feel pretty desperate, and the parents were even more desperate. The method of sleep training that had worked for so many other babies was not working here, so I suggested to his mother that we should try not going in to him at all when he started crying, unless he got into difficulties.

He woke up on the dot of 1:00 A.M., and went berserk; for over an hour he never gave up once. Eventually he went quiet, only to start yelling again an hour later. This went on and off until 5:00 A.M., when he went quiet, and this time he did not wake at 7:00 A.M. I got him up anyway, to try and keep him on track with his daytime sleep. That day saw a vast improvement; he only complained for a few minutes when going down for his naps, and at lunchtime woke up only briefly and settled himself back. That night we agreed to take the same approach: I would only go to him if he got into serious difficulties. He woke twice for approximately 40 minutes each time, but would settle himself back to sleep. For the next three days I stuck rigidly to his daytime routine and did not go to him at all when he woke up during his naps or nighttime sleep. Each day and night the yelling got less and less, and by the fourth night, he fed at 11:00 P.M. and slept straight through until 7:00 A.M.

Having conquered the sleeping, James' mother asked me if I would stay on a further week to try and sort out his feeding. I have to admit I was none too keen, as he was such a demanding baby. But deep down I knew that if the problem of his refusing solids was not sorted out, his sleeping would eventually backtrack again. I agreed to stay for a further week, but on the condition that I did not have to entertain him every waking hour.

By not feeding James milk in the night, I had reduced his daily milk intake to 38 oz. But I realized that to get him interested in solids, I would have to reduce it even further, to around 32 oz. I did not want to cut back on his 10:30 P.M. feed just yet, for fear he would wake up in the night again, so I decided to reduce the 2:30 P.M. feed to 4 oz. He was so hungry by the 6:00 P.M. feed, that he drank 8 oz within ten minutes and took a small amount of rice cereal mixed with a further 1 oz of formula. Normally I would start to introduce rice cereal at the 11:00 A.M. feeding, but because I felt James would have to be really hungry to accept solids, I continued increasing the rice cereal at the 6:00 P.M. feeding.

Within four to five days of gradually increasing the amount of rice cereal plus some pear purée at the 6:00 P.M. feeding, he started to cut right back on his 10:30 P.M. feeding. By the end of the week, he was drinking only 2 oz of formula at that feed, and still sleeping through to 7:00 A.M., so I felt confident that we could drop the 10:30 P.M. feeding. Dropping it would also result in increase his appetite during the day, allowing me to introduce some puréed vegetables after the 11:00 A.M. bottle.

During the final week I spent hours upon hours cooking and puréeing over 80 lb of fruit and vegetables, optimistic that James would eventually grow to love his food. It was also a perfect way of keeping myself so busy that I did not have time to pick James up every time he yelled. With a little help from Madonna and Mozart, he learned to kick and roll and play happily on the floor.

Years later, his mother informs me what a happy, contented little boy he is, who sleeps well and enjoys a very healthy varied diet. Those very traumatic first six months could have been avoided altogether, if the innocent mother had not been misguided by her young maternity nurse. She advised that demand feeding was best, and that a baby should be allowed to find its own sleep pattern.

Routine for a baby
at six to nine months

Feeding times	Nap times between 7:00 A.M. and 7:00 P.M.
7:00 A.M.	9:00 A.M. to 9:30–9:45 A.M.
11:45 A.M.	12:30 P.M. to 2:30 P.M.
2:30 P.M.	
5:00 P.M.	
6:30 P.M.	**MAXIMUM DAILY SLEEP 3 HOURS**

7:00 A.M.

- **Baby should be awake, diaper changed and feeding no later than 7:00 A.M.**
- He should feed from both breasts or have a full bottle, followed by breakfast cereal mixed with either expressed milk or formula and fruit.
- He should stay awake for two hours.

8:00 A.M.

- He should be encouraged to play on his play mat for 20–30 minutes.
- Wash and dress baby, remembering to cream all his creases and dry skin.

9:00 A.M.

- **Settle the drowsy baby, in his sleeping bag (see page 128) in the dark with the door shut and no later than 9:00 A.M.**
- He needs a sleep of 30–45 minutes.

9:30–9:45 A.M.

- Open the curtains and undo his sleeping bag so that he can wake up naturally.

10:00 A.M.

- **Baby must be fully awake now regardless of how long he slept.**
- Encourage him to kick under his play gym or take him on an outing.

11:45 A.M.

- He should be given most of his solids before being offered a drink of water or well-diluted juice from a cup, then alternate between solids and a drink.
- Encourage him to sit in his chair while you clear away the lunch things.

12:20 P.M.

- Check the sheet and change his diaper.
- **Close the curtains and settle the drowsy baby, in his sleeping bag in the dark with the door shut and no later than 12:30 P.M.**

12:30 P.M. to 2:30 P.M.

- **He will need a nap now of no longer than two hours from the time he went down.**
- If he slept the full 45 minutes earlier, he may need less sleep at this nap.

2:30 P.M.

- **Baby must be awake and feeding no later than 2:30 P.M. regardless of how long he has slept.**
- Open the curtains, and allow him to wake up naturally. Change his diaper.
- He needs a feed from both breasts or a full bottle.
- **Do not feed him after 3:15 P.M., as it will put him off his next feed.**

4:15 P.M.

- Change baby's diaper, and offer him a drink of cool boiled water or well-diluted juice no later than 4:30 P.M.

5:00 P.M.

- He should be given most of his solids before being offered a small drink of water from a cup. It is important that he still has a good milk feed at bedtime, so keep this drink to a minimum.

6:00 P.M.

- He must start his bath no later than 6:00 P.M. and be massaged and dressed no later than 6:30 P.M.

6:30 P.M.

- **Baby must be feeding no later than 6:30 P.M.** He should feed from both breasts or have 7 oz of formula.
- Dim the lights and sit him in his chair for ten minutes while you tidy up.

7:00 P.M.

- **Settle baby in his crib and in the dark with the door shut, no later than 7:00 P.M.**

Changes to be made during the six- to nine-month routine

Sleep

Some babies cut right back on their morning nap and may need to be put down to sleep later, but it should be not later than 9:30 A.M. He may also start to roll on to his front and prefer to sleep on his tummy.

Feeding

When protein is introduced at lunchtime, the milk feed should be replaced with a drink of water or well-diluted juice from a cup. Once he drops the lunchtime milk feed, he may need to increase the 2:30 P.M. milk feed. He should be encouraged to take most of his drinks from a cup.

Development and social time

Some babies will attempt to crawl now, and this can be encouraged by placing toys where they can see them, but a little out of reach. Your baby may be able to sit unsupported for short spells at this age, and he will begin to develop a pincer grip, that is using finger and thumb to pick up small objects. He will join in a conversation, with lots of babbling and shouting, and will enjoy songs that involve actions. He should start teething now, and will put everything in his mouth. Now is the time to buy your baby a toothbrush and introduce cleaning teeth into the morning and bedtime routine. Contrary to common belief, teething should not cause sleepless nights or tummy upsets.

Eliza and Emily: aged six months

These twin girls suffered from severe eczema, and their cheeks were so raw that at times they would bleed. It was so bad that it actually looked as if they had been burned with a hot iron. The mother also suffered from severe eczema and was desperate to minimize the pain she knew it could cause, so for six months she exclusively breast-fed both babies, in the hope that it would help.

When the babies were weaned onto solids, she sought the best possible advice from leading nutritionists and dermatologists. By the time she contacted me, she was so physically and mentally exhausted from breast-feeding on demand night and day that she decided to give it up. I supported her decision totally as the eczema was so bad that formula milk could not make it any worse. Also, realistically, I do not think any human being could continue to survive on the small amount of sleep she and her husband were getting. However, there was a major problem: both babies simply refused to feed from a bottle.

I knew from past experience that this could be a very difficult problem to solve. The one thing in our favor was the babies' age, as they were both old enough to last a reasonable period of time without a breast-feed. I agreed to move into their very small one-bedroom apartment on the condition that their mother did not allow either baby on the breast, from 11:00 A.M. that day. I arrived at 6:00 P.M. in the evening and both babies were screaming the place down with hunger, as they had been used to feeding every two to three hours. Their mother had followed my instructions and not fed the babies, and we proceeded to attempt to feed them with expressed milk from a bottle. Eliza fought the bottle, but we did manage to get her to drink a small amount of milk. Emily screamed and fought the bottle so much that she drank nothing. I realized that I had a very tough night ahead of me, so I suggested to their mother that we allow Eliza the remainder of her feeding from the breast. Hopefully she would settle for a few hours, allowing me to concentrate on Emily, whom I figured was going to be the bigger challenge.

We settled both babies in bed by 7:00 P.M., and continued the weaning process. The advice she had received from the dietician was excellent; my only criticism was that there was no structure for the milk feeds. This, in addition to the irritation of the eczema, was the main reason the babies were waking up. I was convinced that their exhausted mother could not to be producing enough milk for them both to get through the night.

Eliza slept through until 3:00 A.M. at which time with a bit of a struggle I managed to get her to drink 3 oz of formula. She settled back to sleep until 6:30 A.M. Emily was much more difficult because she had not had a proper milk feed since 2:00 P.M., and so was very unsettled the whole night. I was concerned that she should not become dehydrated, so I resorted to spooning milk into her whenever she woke up, which was roughly every hour. By 5:00 A.M. the following morning she had only drunk a total of 6 oz of milk since her last breast-feed at 2:00 P.M. the previous day. I knew that if she did not take a reasonable amount from a bottle soon, I would have to give up and allow her a breast-feed. I gave her a pacifier to keep her calm while I heated up the bottle, but she was so exhausted that she started to fall asleep. When the formula was the right temperature, I quickly replaced the pacifier with the bottle and she took 7 oz without stopping. I was so concerned that she would throw it all up that I continued to hold her upright in my arms until 6:30 A.M., when Eliza awoke.

Both the mother and I agreed that now Emily had taken a full feed from the bottle, it was better to keep on with the bottle and not to let her have the breast again. Neither of us felt we would have the strength to cope with a repeat of the previous night; the sanity of the family as a whole depended on both the parents and the babies getting some sleep. Continuing to breast-feed was not an option the mother could even consider at this stage, so the breast milk she was producing had to be reduced gradually. With our experience of how each baby had responded to the bottle, we decided that it would be easier to allow Eliza to reduce the milk supply by going gradually from breast to bottle. If Emily was allowed on the breast again, it might prove even more difficult to persuade her to take the bottle.

By the end of the first week, Emily was having three good bottle-feeds a day, and had taken happily to the cup at the lunchtime feed. Eliza was now on a breast-feed in the morning and one in the evening. She would *also drink happily from a cup at lunchtime, and take a small bottle of formula at the 2:30 P.M. feed. As with all my babies, I kept the 2:30 P.M. feed smaller, to ensure they both fed well at 6:00 P.M. Giving too large a feed at 2:30 P.M., or feeding later than 6:30 P.M. in the day, are major contributory factors in most sleeping and feeding problems.*

The mother's milk supply diminished very quickly, and I was convinced that she probably had not produced enough at the 6:00 P.M. feed to satisfy two babies. They were now both on track with their milk feeding and solids, and I felt confident that it was time to tackle the night waking. This was down to once a night, normally around 3:00 A.M. As their day feeding had improved, they had graduated from sugar water to plain, cool boiled water. Emily normally woke first, and I was sure that it was her crying that caused Eliza to wake. On the tenth night I decided that I was going to let them settle themselves back to sleep when they awoke. Emily woke as usual on the dot of 3:00 A.M. screaming, and was joined very soon by Eliza. Both babies screamed on and off for over an hour, before settling back to sleep until 6:40 A.M. The second night Emily woke again at 3:00 A.M., but this time settled back to sleep within 25 minutes. Eliza stirred when she heard Emily crying but did not wake up, and both babies had to be woken at 7:00 A.M. On the third night both babies slept right through until 7:00 A.M. I did hear them stirring between 3:00 A.M. and 4:00 A.M., but neither of them cried.

They both continued to sleep well at nights, but the lunchtime nap was more difficult to crack. It took over a month to establish a really good nap, as both babies would wake up crying when they came into their light sleep 45 minutes after going to sleep. Eventually I persuaded the mother to hang a piece of blackout lining over the window, as I felt the light shining through the very thin blind did not help. There was an immediate improvement, and although they still woke up, they settled back to sleep much sooner.

I am pleased to say that within a month there was also a slight improvement in their eczema. Five years later both girls are still sleeping well. They both still suffer from eczema, but the mother manages to control it with the use of creams and by watching their diet and ensuring their bedding is free from house mites.

Routine for a baby
at nine to twelve months

Feeding times	Nap times between 7:00 A.M. and 7:00 P.M.
7:00 A.M.	9:00 A.M. to 9:45 A.M.
11:45 A.M.	12:30 P.M. to 2:30 P.M.
2:30 P.M.	
5:00 P.M.	
6:30 P.M.	**MAXIMUM DAILY SLEEP 3 HOURS**

7:00 A.M.

- **Baby should be awake, diaper changed and feeding no later than 7:00 A.M.**
- He should feed from both breasts or have a drink of formula from a cup, followed by breakfast cereal mixed with either expressed milk or formula and fruit.
- He should stay awake for two to two and a half hours.

8:00 A.M.

- He should be encouraged to kick on his play mat for 20–30 minutes.
- Wash and dress baby, remembering to cream all his creases and dry skin.

9:00 A.M.

- **Settle baby in the dark with the door shut no later than 9:30 A.M.** He needs a sleep of 30–45 minutes.

9:30–9:45 A.M.

- Open the curtains so that he can wake up naturally.

10:00 A.M.

- **Baby must be fully awake now regardless of how long he slept.**
- Encourage him to play under his play gym or take him on an outing.

11:45 A.M.

- He should be given most of his solids before being offered a drink of water or well-diluted juice from a cup, then alternate between solids and a drink.
- Encourage him to sit in his chair while you clear away the lunch things.

12:20 P.M.

- Check the sheet and change his diaper.
- Close the curtains and **settle baby, in the dark with the door shut, no later than 12:30 P.M.**

12:30 P.M. to 2:30 P.M.

- **He will need a nap now of no longer than two hours from the time he went down.**
- If he slept the full 45 minutes earlier, he may need less sleep at this nap.

2:30 P.M.

- **Baby must be awake and feeding no later than 2:30 P.M. regardless of how long he has slept.**
- Open the curtains, and allow him to wake naturally. Change his diaper.
- He needs a breast-feed or a drink of formula, water or well-diluted juice from a cup.
- **Do not feed him after 3:15 P.M., as it will put him off his next feed.**

4:15 P.M.

- Change baby's diaper, and offer him a drink of cool boiled water or well-diluted juice no later than 4:30 P.M.

5:00 P.M.

- He should be given most of his solids before being offered a small drink of water or milk from a cup. It is important that he still has a good milk feed at bedtime, so keep this drink to a minimum.

6:00 P.M.

- He must start his bath no later than 6:00 P.M., and be massaged and dressed no later than 6:30 P.M.

6:30 P.M.

- **Baby must be feeding no later than 6:30 P.M.**
- He should feed from both breasts or 7 oz of formula. This will eventually reduce to 5–6 oz when a cup is introduced at one year.
- Dim the lights and sit him in his chair for ten minutes while you tidy up.

7:00 P.M.

- Settle him in his crib, in the dark with the door shut, no later than 7:00 P.M.

Changes to be made during the nine- to twelve-month routine

Sleep

Some babies cut right back on their morning nap and may need to be put down to sleep later, but it should be no later than 9:30 A.M. Your baby may also start to roll on to his front and prefer to sleep on his tummy.

Feeding

When protein is introduced at lunchtime, the milk feed should be replaced with a drink of water or well-diluted juice from a cup. If your baby starts to cut back on his last milk feed, reduce or cut out the 2:30 P.M. feed. Many babies cut out the 2:30 P.M. feed by one year. He should be well on the way to eating most of the meals now. He should also be able to feed himself some of the time. By the age of one year, he should be drinking all his fluids from a cup.

Development and social time

By one year most babies are capable of pulling themselves up, using the crib bars or furniture. Between nine and twelve months your baby will be able to walk if his hands are held. Some babies may even be able to take several steps unaided. He will start to use naming words such as "Mommy," "Daddy," "juice," "book," etc., and his favorite games will be emptying and filling things and throwing things down.

Lucy: aged nine months

Lucy was a third baby and was totally breast-fed. She would not settle at 7:00 P.M., and it would often take three hours of feeding and rocking before she went off to sleep. She would then wake several more times in the night, and need to be breast-fed to get back to sleep. I agreed to move in for six days to try and help sort Lucy out, on the one condition that the mother was prepared to allow controlled crying. I also insisted that Lucy be given a bottle of formula at 7:00 P.M. instead of the breast, as I was convinced that she was probably not getting enough to drink at that feed. Reluctantly her mother agreed to this.

On the first night she took 7 oz of formula, and settled well at 7:30 P.M. At 8:15 P.M. she came into a light sleep and whimpered on and off for ten minutes. Her mother was very anxious and felt we should check her, and I agreed to this as I wanted to see how her mother normally dealt with the situation. On entering the room she switched the lights on, and as Lucy had rolled on to her tummy her mother proceeded to roll her over on to her back again. I explained that a baby of Lucy's age must be allowed to sleep in the position that she finds the most comfortable. She was very concerned about crib death, but agreed to allow Lucy to sleep on her tummy once she had read the literature from The SIDS Foundation (see Useful addresses).

I also reassured her mother that we knew that Lucy had been well fed, so when she woke in the night I would settle her with water. She stirred several times in the night, whimpering but never crying. We had to wake her at 7:00 A.M., and because her mother had not been feeding her on and off all night, she enjoyed a very big breast-feed. I explained that at nine months Lucy did not need to be breast-fed at lunchtime; once protein is introduced at lunchtime, the milk feed should be replaced with a drink of water or well-diluted juice from a cup. Lucy slept well after her lunch, and had the next breast-feed at 2:30 P.M. I knew her mother was very keen to continue breast-feeding, so I suggested that she give Lucy both breasts after her snack at 5:00 P.M. However, I felt it was important to give Lucy a little formula at bedtime.

As on the previous night, she drank 7 oz of formula and settled well. She stirred several times during the night, but only whimpered, never cried. During my six-night stay I never had to go to Lucy once, and each night she slept from 7:30 P.M. to 7:00 A.M.

While her mother was obviously not producing enough milk to settle Lucy at 7:00 P.M., I feel much of the night waking was brought on by her mother rushing to Lucy every time she came into a light sleep and chattered or whimpered. Lucy obviously preferred sleeping on her tummy and rolled over when she came into the light sleep. By forcing Lucy onto her back during this light sleep, her mother was actually waking her up, and the only way to calm her down was to put her to the breast.

Introducing solid food

Weaning your baby

When to wean

Next to sleep, weaning is probably the most emotional subject in baby care. Between two and three months, just as you are beginning to see a regular pattern of milk feeding and sleep evolve, someone will bring up the subject of weaning. It is around this age that most babies discover their hands. This can lead to endless sucking, chewing and dribbling. Well-meaning grandparents and friends voice concern that your baby is hungry and not satisfied on milk alone. While this is one of the signs that a baby is ready to be weaned, it is by no means the only indicator. Do not be pressured into giving your baby solids unless you are absolutely sure he is ready.

It takes up to four months for the lining of the baby's stomach to develop and the kidneys to mature enough to cope with the waste products from solid food. If solids are introduced before a baby has the complete set of enzymes required to digest food properly, his digestive system could become damaged. Many experts blame the rapid increase in allergies over the last 20 years on babies being weaned before their digestive system is ready to cope. Most advise that between four and six months is the age suitable to begin weaning the majority of babies. The American Academy of Pediatrics recommends waiting until the baby is six months old. In my experience, I've found that all babies are different and that some may need to be weaned at three months. Weaning should not begin before neuromuscular coordination has developed sufficiently so that he can control his head and neck while sitting upright supported in a chair to be fed. He should also be able to swallow food easily, by moving it from the front of the mouth to the back.

In accordance with published reports and my own personal experience, I hope the following guidelines will help you decide if your baby is ready to be weaned. If your baby is four months old and weighs between 12 and 14 lb, he is probably ready to begin a small amount of solids if he is constantly showing most of the following signs:

- If he has been feeding well and going four hours between feeds during the day, but now gets very irritable and chews his hands an hour or so before his next feed is due.
- He is bottle-fed and taking in more than 38 oz per day but still appears to be hungry after a full feed of 8 oz four times a day.
- He usually sleeps well at night and nap times, but is waking up earlier and earlier.

A baby weighing over 9 lb at birth is most likely to reach 14 lb by three months. If he is showing most of the above signs, he probably needs to be weaned.

Breast-fed babies

With a baby who is being fully breast-fed, it is more difficult to tell how much milk he is receiving. If he is over four months and showing most of the above signs, I would probably wean him.

If he is under four months and not gaining enough weight each week, it is possible that your milk supply is getting very low later in the evening. All that may be needed is extra milk. I suggest you try giving the baby a couple of ounces of formula after the 10:00 P.M. feed. If this does not work or if he is waking up more than once in the night, I would replace the 10:00 P.M. feed altogether with a full bottle-feed. Encourage your partner to do this feed so that you can get to bed early, after expressing whatever milk you have at 9:00 P.M. to avoid your supply dropping any further. Mothers in this situation often find that when they express, they are only producing 3–4 oz, which is much less than what their baby may need at this feed. The milk expressed can, if necessary, be given at some other feed during the day, thus avoiding further complementary bottle-feeding.

This plan usually satisfies the baby's hunger, improves his weight gain and gets him through to four months before you need to introduce solids.

First stage: four to six months

Studies into weaning by the University of Surrey revealed that babies fed diets with a high fruit content may be more prone to diarrhea, which leads to slow growth. They advise that rice cereal is the best first weaning food, as fruit may not be so well tolerated by the underdeveloped intestines of some babies.

Weaning: Days 1–15

Days	Time	Food	Amount	Advice
1–3	11:00 A.M.	rice cereal	1 tsp	mix with milk
4–6	6:00 P.M.	rice cereal	1 tsp	increase a little each day until he is taking 1 full tsp
7–9	11:00 A.M.	pear purée	1 tsp	
	6:00 P.M.	rice cereal	1–2 tsp	increase a little each day until he is taking 2 full tsp
10–12	11:00 A.M.	carrot purée	1 tsp	keep offering milk first
	6:00 P.M.	rice cereal	1–2 tsp	give 7 oz formula, then solids,
		plus pear	1–2 tsp	then offer remaining formula
13–15	11:00 A.M.	apple purée	1–2 tsp	still give milk first
	6:00 P.M.	rice cereal	2–3 tsp	gradually work up to 3 and 4 tsp
		plus pear	2–3 tsp	of rice cereal and 1 cube pear

By 15 days he should be having up to 1 cube of carrot purée at lunch, and up to 3 teaspoons of rice cereal plus 1 cube of pear purée at 6:00 P.M. He should continue to have most of his milk first, at least 7 oz before the solids.

Introduce a further fruit at lunchtime, either apple or peach. After three days transfer to the evening meal and introduce sweet potato with the carrot at lunchtime for a further three days.

Start to alternate the fruit at nighttime. From now on introduce a new vegetable every three days at lunchtime, alternating with the ones he is already eating.

Note: To avoid problems with baby's digestion, new foods must only be introduced every three days.

I always start weaning at the 11:00 A.M. feed with a teaspoon of pure organic rice cereal mixed with either a small amount of the formula or some expressed breast milk. I find it best to give the baby most of his milk feed first, then offer the rice cereal followed by the rest of the milk. Consult your baby's doctor before introducing solids.

It is vital to remember that milk is still the most important food at this stage. By replacing it too quickly with solid food, you will deny your baby the perfect balance of vitamins and minerals that milk supplies. By using the above method during the first weeks of weaning, you can be sure your baby will take exactly the amount of solids that he needs, without losing the nutritional value of the milk.

Once the baby is established on rice cereal at 11:00 A.M. and shows no reaction, I would transfer the cereal to after the 6:00 P.M. feed. I then introduce a teaspoonful of organic pear after the 11:00 A.M. feed. If it is tolerated, after three days I would mix the pear with the cereal at the 6:00 P.M. feed. This makes the cereal more palatable and avoids the baby becoming constipated. I now begin to introduce a small amount of various organic vegetables and fruit after the 11:00 A.M. feed. I am convinced that the reason very few of my babies develop a sweet tooth is because they are given more vegetables than fruit in the early days of weaning. The vegetables favored by most babies at this stage are carrots, sweet potato, green beans, zucchini and turnips.

Other foods

Gillian Harris, a clinical psychologist researching weaning in babies, found that babies introduced to a wide variety of nonallergy-forming foods from the age of four months would accept a wider range of foods at one year than those weaned on a restricted diet. I agree with this, as I have found that babies who are allowed excessive quantities of milk between four and six months and are not encouraged to enjoy solids usually end up very fussy eaters.

Between the ages of five and six months, babies who started weaning at four months should have tasted cereal, plus a variety of vegetables and fruit from the ones listed in the first stage on page 146. Food still needs to be puréed, but not so smoothly. This will help prepare your baby for mashed food at six months.

Meat, chicken or fish should not be introduced until the baby is capable of digesting reasonable amounts of other solids. Some nutritionists believe that protein can put a strain on the young baby's kidneys and digestive tract. I agree with this, as all too often I have seen feeding problems occur because meat, poultry or fish have been introduced too early. A very large baby could start protein at around five months, but for most, six or seven months is the best age.

Dairy products, wheat, eggs, nuts and citrus fruits should still be avoided at this stage, as they are the foods most likely to trigger allergies. Salt should be avoided and sugar only used in small quantities when stewing very sour fruit. Honey should not be introduced before one year.

Breakfast

A baby is ready to start having breakfast once he shows signs of hunger long before his 11:00 A.M. feed. This usually happens between the ages of five and six months. All cereal should be wheat and gluten free until the baby is older. I find that organic oatmeal with a small amount of puréed fruit is a favorite with most babies.

You should still give your baby most of his milk feed first. After a couple of weeks give about two-thirds of his milk feed first, then the cereal, finishing up with the remainder of the milk feed. If your baby reaches six months and shows no sign of wanting breakfast, it would be wise to reduce his milk feed very slightly and offer a small amount of solids.

Daily requirements

By six months most babies are enjoying at least two meals a day and heading toward a third. If your baby is not showing much interest in solids but is drinking a lot of milk, it would be wise to cut back on his lunchtime feed to encourage his interest in the solids. Some babies get really hooked on milk and hate the feel of a spoon in their mouth and start to refuse solid food altogether.

Your baby still needs a minimum of 30 oz of breast or formula milk a day.

Molly: aged six months

Molly was difficult to settle in the evening and would wake up two to three times in the night. She drank very little milk and screamed when fed solids. Because she was very underweight for her age, she had been admitted to a hospital at the age of five months to be tested for the cause of the sleeping and feeding problems. The hospital visit confirmed that there was nothing physically wrong with Molly, but because of her low weight gain the parents were advised to continue to feed little and often, and on demand. She would, they said, "eventually sort herself out." Easy advice to give if you are not the one being deprived of sleep night after night, and trying to cope with a cranky baby and a toddler during the day.

As is my usual practice, I observed the mom and baby the first day. Because of her disruptive nights, Molly normally started her day at 8:30 A.M. She would drink around 3 oz of formula, followed by a small amount of cereal. Molly would then be awake for at least four hours, most of which time was spent whining or crying, and she had to be carried or held the whole time. At 11:00 A.M. she would be given another bottle-feed, then a jar of either chicken casserole or beef stew. As with breakfast she would only take 2 oz of milk and a few spoonfuls of solids before she started screaming and straining. She had suffered from constipation since being weaned at three months.

Her mother would usually end up putting her in her stroller in the kitchen and rocking her to sleep. Molly had never slept more than one hour at this time of the day, and would normally wake up screaming. Her mother, concerned about her low milk intake, immediately would offer her a bottle of formula. This would be her best feed of the day, and she would drink around 6 oz, then fall asleep, exhausted, for at least two hours.

Her older sister arrived home from school around now, and usually managed to keep Molly entertained while their mother made an early supper for both girls. At 4:30 P.M. Molly would have fruit, followed by approximately 4 oz of formula.

Both girls were taken upstairs around 5:30 P.M. for their bath. After the bath, at about 6:30 P.M. Molly was given a bottle, of which she would usually drink 3–4 oz, and fall straight to sleep. She would then wake up two hours later, take a further 2 oz and fall asleep until around one in the morning.

The parents had tried many times to wake her between 10:00 P.M.

and 11:00 P.M. to give her a bottle in the hope that she would sleep through. She was always in such a deep sleep at this time that it was impossible to wake her enough to get her to drink more than 2 oz of formula. There were normally at least two other wakings in the night, and each time she would usually drink no more than 2 oz. Eventually, at 5:00 A.M. Molly would settle into a deep sleep. The parents, exhausted after a night of broken sleep, were so desperate for sleep themselves that they would let her sleep until 8:30 A.M. and on some occasions even 9:00 A.M.

Molly was drinking on average a daily total of 24–26 oz of formula, which in itself would be fairly normal for a baby of her age. The problem was that nearly half of this amount was being drunk between 9:00 P.M. and 5:00 A.M., when she should have been drinking the whole amount between 7:00 A.M. and 7:00 P.M.

The other big concern was that her solid intake was very low, and nutritionally virtually nil. Molly was fed exclusively on jarred baby food with a high water and sugar content. (Jarred baby food in the United States is of a higher quality than is often found in Britain.) It is not surprising that Molly was way below her proper level on her growth chart.

I decided to take Molly right back to stage one of the weaning program. My main aim was to get her to take a full formula feed first thing in the morning and in the evening, and to get used to eating proper food. In order for her to be hungry enough in the morning, I knew I had to get rid of the middle-of-the-night feeding. The first day I cut the 2:30 P.M. feed, which was normally her best, right back to 3 oz and cut out her 4:30 P.M. solids altogether. In the evening after her bath, she took 6 oz, which was more milk than normal. I also gave her two small spoonfuls of rice cereal mixed with 1 oz of formula. She did not wake up at 9:00 P.M., but did wake as usual at 1:00 P.M. and 4:00 P.M. Both times I offered her a small amount of sugared water and cuddled her back to sleep. She awoke at 6:45 A.M., and for the first time ever, very quickly drank a full 8-oz bottle of formula in ten minutes.

I decided not to give her breakfast for a few days until her bottle-feeding and lunch and supper were properly established. At 11:00 A.M., I offered her another 8-oz bottle of formula, of which she took 7 oz, followed by a few spoonfuls of mashed potato and puréed carrot. When she awoke at 2:30 P.M., I gave her a small feed of 5 oz. I knew she would have taken more at this feed, but I deliberately wanted to keep it small, to encourage her to take a really good feed at bedtime.

Around 5:00 P.M. she became very irritable, so I let her suck on a cracker, most of which went on the floor, but it did occupy her until bath time. After the bath at 6:00 P.M. she gulped down 7 oz of formula, followed by rice cereal and fruit purée.

For her sleep pattern that day, I followed the routine for a four-month-old baby; this was to allow her time to settle herself to sleep. Apart from a few brief protests, she adapted to this very well. She yelled for 20 minutes when she went down at 7:00 P.M., and I did not hear another peep until 3:00 A.M. Like the previous night, I offered her sugar water and cuddled her back to sleep. For the following three days I followed much the same routine. She gradually increased her solids until she was eating an acceptable amount for a baby of her age, and she continued to take her bottle well.

By this time she was still waking once in the night, but only taking a small amount of plain, cool boiled water and settling back very quickly. I decided now was the time for her to learn how to settle herself in the night when she woke up. Her daytime naps were on routine and she was feeding well, so I felt confident she would get out of the habit of needing the water very quickly. The first night she cried on and off for 40 minutes, the next night for 30 minutes and the last night 15 minutes. She then slept through from 7:00 P.M. to 6:45 A.M.

Two weeks later we dropped the 11:00 A.M. milk feed and reintroduced chicken casserole for lunch, but we found that she became very constipated again and started to fuss over her food. I suggested that we avoid giving her protein and starch at the same meal, and this seemed to solve that problem.

We also had to continue giving her the solids after the 6:00 P.M. bottle-feed for a further three months. On the couple of occasions we gave her the solids at 5:00 P.M., she refused to drink a full feed at 6:00 P.M. This resulted in a 5:00 A.M. waking, instead of the usual 7:00 A.M.

While Molly did have some wrong sleep association problems, I believe that they were not the main cause of the disruptive nights. I am convinced the real problems were poor structuring of milk feeds and weaning too early on to the wrong type of solid food. I am pleased to say Molly started to gain weight and continued to sleep well.

Second stage: six to nine months

During the first stage of weaning, milk is still providing your baby with all the nutrients he needs. In the second stage of weaning, solids should gradually take over and provide more of your baby's daily nutritional needs. You should be aiming toward three well-balanced meals a day.

Most babies are ready to accept stronger tasting foods at this age. They also take pleasure from different textures, colors and presentation. Foods should be mashed or minced and kept separate so that they avoid mixing everything up. Fruit need not be cooked; it can be grated or mashed. It is also around this age that your baby will begin to put food in his mouth. Raw soft fruit, lightly cooked vegetables and toast can be used as finger foods. They will be sucked and squeezed more than eaten at this stage, but allowing him the opportunity to feed himself encourages good feeding habits later on. Once your baby is having finger foods, always wash his hands before a meal and never leave him alone while he is eating.

Foods to introduce with caution

Chicken, fish and meat can be introduced at this stage. Check that all the bones are removed and trim off the fat and the skin. Some babies find the flavor of protein cooked on its own too strong. Try cooking chicken or meat in a stew, and fish in a milk sauce until your baby becomes accustomed to the different texture and taste.

Dairy products and wheat can also be introduced at this stage. Full-fat cow's milk can be used in cooking, but should not be given as a drink until one year. All these foods should be introduced gradually and careful notes made of any allergic reactions.

Introducing a cup

Once protein is introduced at lunchtime, the milk feed must be replaced by a drink of water or well-diluted juice from a cup. Most babies of six months are capable of sipping and swallowing, and this should be encouraged by being consistent and always offering the lunchtime drink from a cup. Do not worry if your baby only drinks a small amount at this meal. You will probably find that he makes up for it at his 2:30 P.M. milk feed.

Breakfast

Sugar-free, unrefined wheat cereals can now be introduced; choose ones fortified with iron and B vitamins. Try adding a little mashed or grated fruit if your baby refuses them. You can encourage your baby with finger foods by offering him a little buttered toast at this stage. Most babies are still desperate for their milk first thing in the morning, so still allow him two-thirds of his milk first.

Lunch

At this stage most babies are eating a proper breakfast, and lunch comes a little later, somewhere between 11:45 A.M. and 12:00 noon. Once you introduce chicken or fish at lunchtime, you should replace the milk feed with a drink of water or well-diluted juice from a cup. Encourage your baby to take most of his solids before offering him a drink. He needs one portion of protein a day, and lentils and other beans are good alternatives to chicken or fish.

Dinner

During the second stage of weaning, the rice and fruit that has been given after the 6:00 P.M. milk feed will be replaced with dinner at 5:00 P.M. This can consist of foods like mini sandwiches, or a baked potato or pasta served with vegetables and a sauce. Some babies get very tired and fussy by dinner. If you always make sure your baby has a well-balanced breakfast and lunch, you can be more relaxed about this meal. If your baby does not eat much, try offering some rice pudding or a yogurt. A small drink of water from a cup can be offered after the meal. Do not allow too large a drink at this time, as it will put him off his last milk feed.

His bedtime milk feed is still important at this stage. If he starts cutting back too much on this feed, check you are not overfeeding him on solids.

Daily requirements

At this stage your baby should be well on the way to eating three proper meals a day. They should include two to three servings of carbohydrates, such as cereals, bread and pasta, plus at least two servings of vegetables and fruit, and one serving of puréed meat, fish or beans. By six months a baby has used up all the store of iron he was born with. As his requirements between 6 and 12 months are particularly high, it is important that his diet provides the right amount of iron. To help improve iron absorption in cereals and meat, always serve with fruit or vegetables and avoid giving milk to drink with protein, as it reduces the iron absorption by 50 percent.

He still needs 18–20 oz of breast or formula milk a day inclusive of milk used for mixing food. If your baby starts to reject his milk, try giving him more cheese, milk sauces and yogurt.

Third stage: nine to twelve months

Between nine and twelve months your baby should be eating and enjoying all types of food, with the exception of food with a high fat, salt or sugar content. Peanuts and honey should also still be avoided. It is very important that your baby learns to chew properly at this stage. Food should be chopped or diced, although meat will still need to be mashed or very finely chopped. This is also a good time to introduce raw vegetables and salads.

Try to include some finger foods at every meal, and if he shows an interest in holding his own spoon, do not discourage these attempts. It is important that he enjoys his meals, even if a certain amount of it lands on the floor. Always supervise your baby while he is feeding himself.

Breakfast

Encourage your baby to take at least some of his breakfast milk feed from a cup. By the end of the first year he should be drinking all of his breakfast milk from a cup. Aim to get him to take 7 oz of milk at this meal, divided between a drink and his breakfast cereal. Scrambled eggs can be offered once or twice a week as a change.

Lunch

Lunch should consist of a wide selection of lightly steamed, chopped vegetables served with a daily serving of meat or meat alternative. Babies of this age are very active and can become quite tired and irritable by 5:00 P.M. By ensuring a well-balanced lunch, you will not need to worry if dinner is more relaxed. By the end of the first year, your baby's lunch can be integrated with the family lunch, so prepare the meal without salt, sugar or spices and reserve a portion for the baby, then add the desired flavorings for the rest of the family.

Try to ensure that his meals are attractively presented, with a variety of different colored vegetables and fruit. Do not overload his plate; serve up a small amount and when he finishes that, replenish his plate. This also helps to avoid the game of throwing his food on the floor, which often occurs at this stage. If your baby does start to play with his main course, refusing to eat and throwing his food on the floor, quietly and firmly say no, and remove the plate. Do not offer him a cookie half an hour later, as a pattern will soon emerge where he will refuse his lunch, knowing he will get something sweet if he acts up enough. A piece of fruit can be offered mid-afternoon to see him through to his dinner, at which time he will probably eat very well.

A drink of well-diluted, pure unsweetened orange juice in a cup will help the absorption of iron at this meal, but make sure that he has most of his meal before you allow him to finish the drink.

Dinner

Many babies cut out their 2:30 P.M. milk during this stage. If you are worried that your baby's daily milk intake is too low, try giving things like pasta and vegetables with a milk sauce, baked potatoes with grated cheese, cheesy vegetable bake or mini quiches at dinner. Dinner is usually the meal when I would give small helpings of pudding or yogurt, which are also alternatives if milk is being rejected. Try regularly to include some finger foods at dinner.

The bedtime bottle should be discouraged after one year, so during this stage get your baby gradually used to less milk at bedtime. This can be done by offering him a small drink of milk with his last meal, then a drink of 5–6 oz of milk from a cup at bedtime.

Daily requirements

By one year it is important that large volumes of milk are discouraged; no more than 20 oz inclusive of milk used in food should be allowed. After one year your baby needs a minimum of 11¼ oz a day. This is usually divided between two or three drinks and inclusive of milk used in cooking or on cereals.

Full-fat, pasteurized cow's milk can be given to drink after one year. If your baby refuses cow's milk, try gradually diluting his formula with it until he is happy to take full cow's milk. If possible try to give your baby organic cow's milk, as it comes from cows fed exclusively on grass, unlike some unorganic milk, where the cows are fed synthetic growth hormones.

Encourage three well-balanced meals a day and avoid snacks of cookies, cakes and chips.

Your questions answered

Q **At what age would you wean a baby onto solids?**

A • The majority of babies do not need solid food before four to six months.
   • Occasionally a larger baby weighing more than 14 lb at three months may need to be weaned earlier.
   • If I do have to wean a baby before four months, I keep the food very simple until he reaches four months, i.e. pure organic rice cereal and puréed organic pear.

Q **How will I know when my baby is ready to be weaned?**

A • If your baby has been sleeping through and starts to wake up in the night or very early in the morning and will not settle back to sleep.
   • A bottle-fed baby is taking in excess of 32 oz to 38 oz a day, draining an 8-oz bottle each feed and looking for another feed long before it is due.
   • A breast-fed baby would start to look for a feed every two to three hours.
   • Both breast- and bottle-fed babies would start to chew on their hands a lot and be very irritable in between feeds.
   • If unsure, always talk to your pediatrician.

Q **What would happen if I weaned my baby before he was ready?**

A • His digestive system could be harmed if he has not developed the complete set of enzymes required to digest solids.
   • Introducing solids before he is ready could lead to allergies.
   • Studies from several different countries show that persistent coughs and wheezing are more common in babies who were weaned before 12 weeks.

Q   At which milk feed should I introduce solids?

A • I usually start at the 11:00 A.M. feed as this feed will gradually be pushed to 12:00 noon, becoming a proper lunch once solids become established.

  • Milk is still the most important source of food. By giving solids after this feed, you can be sure that your baby will have at least half of his daily milk intake before noon.

  • Solids offered at the 2:30 P.M. feed seem to put babies off the very important 6:00 P.M. feed.

  • If a very hungry baby has no reaction to the rice cereal within three days, I would then transfer the cereal to after the 6:00 P.M. feed.

Q   Which is the best food to introduce?

A • I find pure organic rice cereal is the food that satisfies most baby's hunger the best. If this is tolerated, I would then introduce some organic puréed pear.

  • Once these two foods are established, it is best to concentrate on introducing a variety of vegetables from the first stage on p. 146.

  • In a survey carried out by the University of Surrey, it was found that babies weaned on fruit were less likely to thrive than those weaned on rice cereal. They advise that all babies should start weaning on rice cereal.

Q   How will I know how much solid food to give my baby?

A • For the first six months, milk is still the most important part of your baby's diet. It will provide him with the right balance of vitamins and minerals, so he will need a minimum of 20 oz a day. During the first month of weaning, if you always offer the milk feed first, then the solids, you can be sure he will take exactly the amount of solids he needs. This avoids him replacing his milk too quickly with solids.

  • Between five and six months you can start at the 11:00 A.M. feed to give half the milk feed first, then some solids followed by more milk. This will encourage your baby to cut back slightly on his milk feed and increase his solids, preparing him for a feeding pattern of three meals a day at six months.

  • With breast-fed babies a feed from one breast can be classed as half a milk feed.

Q   At what age should I start to reduce the amount of milk he drinks?

A • Up to the age of six months your baby still needs a minimum of 20 oz of milk a day. From five months more milk will be used to mix his cereal and solids, so the actual amount he drinks reduces slightly, but his daily intake should remain much the same.

• As he increases his solids, the feeds he should cut back on are the 11:00 A.M. and 2:30 P.M.

• Your baby should be established on the tier system at lunchtime by six months.

• Once your baby is established on three meals a day, introduce the tier-system breakfast (see p. 128).

Q   At what age do I start to cut out milk feeds altogether?

A • Assuming your baby was on five milk feeds when he started to wean, once he increases his solids after the 6:00 P.M. feed, he should automatically cut back on his 10:00 P.M. feed, and cut it out altogether somewhere between four and five months.

• The next feed to cut out would be the 11:00–11:30 A.M. feed. Once your baby is having chicken or fish for lunch, the milk feed should be replaced with a drink of water or well-diluted juice from a cup.

• The 2:30 P.M. feed often increases for a few months, then somewhere between nine and twelve months he will lose interest in this feed, at which time it can be dropped.

Q   At what age would you introduce a drinking cup and at which feeds?

A • Between the ages of six and seven months is the best time.

• When you have replaced the lunchtime milk feed with water or well-diluted juice, try giving it from a cup or a bottle with a hard spout.

• Try halfway through the meal and after every few spoonfuls of food.

• It is important to persevere. Experiment with different types of cup until you find one with which your baby is happy.

• Once he is taking a few ounces from a cup, gradually introduce it at other feeds.

• Most health advisers recommend that bottle-feeding is discouraged after one year, as it will stop the appetite for other foods.

Q   When can I introduce cow's milk?

A • I usually introduce a small amount of organic cow's milk in cooking from six months.

   • Cow's milk should not be given as a drink until your baby is at least one year old.

   • It should always be full-fat pasteurized milk.

   • If your baby refuses cow's milk, try mixing half the amount with formula. Once he is happy taking that, gradually increase the cow's milk until he is happy with all cow's milk.

Q   At what age can I stop puréeing his food?

A • Around the age of six to seven months I start to mash the vegetables and fruit really well, so that there are no lumps, but it is not as smooth as the puréed food.

   • Between six and nine months I gradually mash the food less and less until the baby will take food with lumps in it.

   • Chicken and meat should still be minced until your baby is around ten months old.

Q   When will he be able to manage finger foods?

A • From six months of age most babies are capable of eating a small amount of finger foods.

   • He should be offered small pieces of softly cooked vegetables or pieces of soft fruit.

   • Once he is managing vegetables and fruit, offer a piece of toast or a rice cracker.

   • By nine months encourage a variety of lightly cooked or raw foods, in the form of finger foods or chopped with his main meal.

Q   At what age will he be able to feed himself with a spoon?

A • Once your baby starts to grab at the spoon, give him one to hold.

   • When he repeatedly puts it in his mouth, load up another spoon and let him try to get it into his mouth, quickly popping in any food that falls out with your spoon.

   • With a little help and guidance most babies from 12 months are capable of feeding themselves with part of their meal.

   • Always supervise your baby during mealtimes. Never, ever leave him alone.

Q   When can I stop sterilizing?

A   • Bottles should be sterilized until your baby is one year old.*

   • Dishes and spoons can stop being sterilized when your baby is six months. They can then be put in the dishwasher, or washed thoroughly in hot soapy water, then rinsed and left to air dry.

   • Between four and six months, the pots and cooking utensils used for preparing weaning food can either be put in the dishwasher or washed in hot soapy water, rinsed and then have boiled water poured over them before being left to air dry.

Q   Which foods are most likely to cause allergies and what are the main symptoms?

A   • The most common foods that cause allergies are dairy products, wheat, fish, eggs and citrus fruits.

   • Symptoms include rashes, wheezing, coughing, running nose, sore bottom, diarrhea, irritability and swelling of the eyes.

   • Keeping a detailed record when you are weaning can be a big help when you are trying to establish the cause of any of the above symptoms.

   • The above symptoms can also be caused by house mites, animal fur, wool and certain soaps and household cleaning agents.

   • If in doubt, always check with your doctor to rule out any other possible causes or illness for the above symptoms.

Feeding plan at four to five months

	Week 1	Week 2	Week 3	Week 4
Introduce	Rice cereal	Apple	Sweet potato	Zucchini
	Pear	Carrot	Green beans	Turnip

   • When preparing food, always ensure that all surfaces are clean and have been wiped down with an antibacterial cleaner. Use paper towels for cleaning surfaces and drying, as it is more hygienic than dishcloths and sponges, which may carry bacteria.

---

* Editor's Note: Other parenting and child care sources in the United States say: Bottles and feeding equipment should be sterilized until the baby is three months old. You can use a bottle sterilizer, stove top or dishwasher set at high heat.

- All fresh fruit and vegetables should be carefully peeled, removing the core, seeds and any blemishes. They should then be rinsed thoroughly.
- All fruit and vegetables must be cooked until your baby is six months old. This can be done by either steaming or boiling. Do not add salt, sugar or honey.
- At this stage all food must be cooked until soft enough to purée to a very smooth consistency. A small amount of the cooking water may need to be added so that the mixture is similar to smooth yogurt.
- If using a food processor, check carefully for lumps by using a spoon and pouring into another bowl. Then transfer to ice cube trays or containers for storage in the freezer.
- Freshly prepared food should be cooled quickly and put in the freezer or fridge as soon as possible after cooking.
- Whether using fresh produce, packets or jars, try whenever possible to buy organic produce, which is free from preservatives and pesticides. Avoid store-bought processed food with artificial flavorings, added sugars or fillers.
- Introduce solids after the 11:00 A.M. feed. Prepare in advance everything needed for giving the solids: baby chair, two bibs, two spoons and a clean, fresh damp cloth.
- Always offer the milk first, as milk is still the most important food at this stage. It provides your baby's nutritional needs with the right balance of vitamins and minerals.
- Solids at this stage are only first tastes and fillers, which prepare your baby for three meals a day. His daily milk intake should not decrease at this stage.
- Food should be heated thoroughly to ensure that any bacteria are killed. If using jars, always transfer to a dish; never serve straight from the jar. Any food left over should be discarded, never reheated and used again.
- Make sure food is cooled enough before feeding it to your baby.
- Use a shallow plastic spoon, never a metal one, which can be too sharp or get too hot.
- Some babies need help in learning how to feed from the spoon. By placing the spoon just far enough into his mouth and bringing the spoon up and out against the roof of his mouth, his upper gums will take off the food, encouraging him to feed.
- Always be very positive and smile when offering new foods. If

your baby spits it out, it may not mean he dislikes it. This is all very new to him, and different foods get different reactions. If he positively refuses a food, leave it and try again in a week.

- Introduce a new food every three to four days so that you can see how your baby reacts to each new food.
- Encourage more vegetables than fruit, but avoid strong-tasting ones like broccoli and spinach at this stage. Concentrate on the root vegetables listed in the feeding plan, which are naturally sweeter.
- By the end of six months lunch should be made up of a selection of vegetables and sweet potato. Supper would be organic rice cereal and fruit purée.
- Be guided by your baby as to when to increase the amounts. He will turn his head away and get fussy when he has had enough.
- He still needs a minimum of 20 oz a day of breast milk or formula, so keep giving him the milk first to ensure that you do not increase solids too quickly.
- Encourage him to sit in his chair and entertain himself while you clear up. Any cloths used to wash his face and hands should be put in the wash with the bibs to avoid bacteria buildup.
- By five months his day's menu may look something like the following:

Breakfast Breast-feed or 6–8 oz of formula milk

Lunch Breast-feed or 6–8 oz of formula milk
Sweet potato with one other vegetable

Afternoon Breast-feed or 5–7 oz of formula milk

Evening Breast-feed or 7–8 oz formula milk
Rice cereal with a small amount of fruit purée

Feeding plan at five to six months

	Week 1	Week 2	Week 3	Week 4
Introduce	Oats	Parsnip	Mango	Peas
	Peaches	Avocado	Barley	Cauliflower

- All fruit and vegetables should still be steamed or cooked in water until soft, then puréed. Mix to the desired consistency with some of the cooking water, or chicken stock may be used with vegetables.

- Introduce some oat cereal mixed with some of your baby's first milk feed and fruit purée for breakfast.
- Once breakfast is introduced, he should be happy to go longer between his feeds. Gradually keep pushing the 11:00 A.M. feed later until he is eating lunch between 11:45 A.M. and 12:00 noon.
- Once he is eating lunch at a later time, you can start to use the tier method of feeding (see p. 128), alternating between his milk and the solids.
- Once the tier method of eating is introduced at lunchtime, the solids should start to overtake the milk. Keep increasing the solids and gradually reduce the milk feed, preparing him to drop it once protein is introduced.
- In the evening make sure he still has at least 7–8 oz of formula or both breasts for his last feed at 6:00–7:00 P.M.
- Milk intake may have dropped slightly, but he still needs a minimum of 20 oz a day of breast or formula milk.
- By six months his day's menu may look something like the following:

Breakfast Breast-feed or 7–8 oz of formula
Oat cereal with fruit purée

Lunch Breast-feed or 5–7 oz of formula
Potato or barley cereal mixed with a selection of other vegetables

Afternoon Breast-feed or 5–6 oz of formula

Evening Breast-feed or 7–8 oz of formula
Baby rice or gluten-free cereal with a small amount of fruit purée

Feeding plan at six to seven months

Introduce	Week 1	Week 2	Week 3	Week 4
	Chicken	Lentils	Cheddar cheese	Fish
	Broccoli	Asparagus	Peas	Bananas
	Yogurt	Wheat	Brown rice	Peppers

- Each day your baby should have two to three servings of carbohydrates in the form of cereal, whole grain bread, pasta or potatoes.
- Cheese should be full fat, pasteurized and grated, and preferably organic.
- Your baby should have at least three servings of vegetables and fruit a day, and he will also need one serving of animal or vegetable protein.
- Meat and poultry should have all fat, skin and bones removed. Cook with vegetables as a stew and pulse in a food processor.
- Vegetables should be mashed now, not puréed, and most fruit can be served raw, either mashed or grated.
- Introduce small amounts of finger foods: cubes of raw soft fruit or cooked vegetables. Once he manages these, toast or rice crackers can also be offered but make sure you wash his hands thoroughly before and after the meal.
- When he is having protein at lunchtime, the milk feed should be replaced with a drink of water or well-diluted juice—try to encourage him to drink from a cup.
- A very hungry baby may need a small drink and a piece of fruit mid-morning. Small amounts of butter and full-fat cow's milk (preferably organic) can be used in cooking, but cow's milk should not be given as a drink yet, as it is too low in iron.
- He still needs 18–20 oz of breast or formula each day, inclusive of milk used in sauces and cereals.
- By the end of six months, your baby will probably be ready to sit in a high chair for his meals.
- If your baby has cut any teeth, they should be cleaned twice a day.
- By seven months his day's menu may look something like the following:

Breakfast   Breast-feed or 7–8 oz of formula
Whole grain or oat cereal with milk and fruit *or*
Baby muesli with milk and fruit
Toast with fruit spread

Lunch   Chicken casserole *or*
Steamed fish with creamed vegetables *or*
Vegetable casserole *or*
Chicken risotto *or*

Chicken with asparagus and peach purée
Drink of water or well-diluted juice from a cup

Mid-afternoon Breast-feed or 5–7 oz of formula

Dinner   Baked potato with creamed vegetables *or*
Pasta and vegetables with a sauce *or*
Thick barley broth *or*
Pasta with red pepper sauce
Bread, zwiebacks or rice cakes with a cheese or
  vegetarian spread
Milk pudding or yogurt
Small drink of water from a cup

Bedtime   Breast-feed or 6–8 oz of formula

Feeding plan at seven to eight months

Introduce	Week 1	Week 2	Week 3	Week 4
	Soya	Lamb	Beans	Cabbage
	Apricots	Melon	Plums	Tomatoes
	Pumpkin	Spinach	Olive oil	Herbs

- Each day your baby should have two to three servings of carbohydrates in the form of cereal, whole grain bread, pasta or potatoes.
- He should also have at least two servings of vegetables and fruit each day and will need one serving of animal protein or two of vegetable protein.
- He should be eating three well-balanced meals a day and drinking three milk feeds from the breast, bottle or cup. The 2:30 P.M. feed should be established from the cup by eight months.
- All fruit and vegetables should be mashed or minced, and dried fruit should be washed thoroughly and soaked first.
- Olive oil can be used when cooking casseroles, and by the end of eight months small quantities of herbs can be used in cooking.
- Continue to offer finger foods such as pieces of raw soft fruits, lightly cooked vegetables and bread, rice crackers or toast with a cheese or vegetarian spread.
- Try to get him to drink all his well-diluted juice or water from a cup. A bottle-fed baby should be encouraged to drink some of his

breakfast milk from a cup, but he still needs to feed from both breasts or have a 6–7-oz bottle-feed at 6:30 P.M.

- If he refuses or cuts right back on his last milk feed, try cutting down on his 2:30 P.M. milk feed. If this fails, replace the 2:30 P.M. feed with well-diluted juice, as if he cuts out a milk feed it is better to do so at 2:30 P.M. than at 6:30 P.M.

- He still needs a minimum of 18–20 oz of breast milk or formula each day. If he is not taking this amount, introduce more cheese sauces, milk puddings or yogurt.

- By eight months his day's menu may look something like the following:

Breakfast   Breast-feed or 6–8 oz of formula
Whole grain or oat cereal with milk and fruit *or*
Baby muesli with milk and fruit *or*
Toast with fruit spread *plus*
Mixed fruit and yogurt

Lunch   Lamb stew with carrot and potato purée *or*
Cod with broccoli and cheese sauce *or*
Lentil and spinach lasagne *or*
Chicken and tomato risotto *or*
Vegetarian hash
Drink of water or well-diluted juice from a cup

Mid-afternoon Breast-feed or 5–7 oz of formula

Dinner   Thick minestrone and pasta soup *or*
Cream of leek and potato soup *plus*
Bread, rice crackers or rice cakes with a cheese or
    vegetarian spread *or*
Lima bean casserole *or*
Spinach and pasta bake
Cottage cheese with fruit or yogurt
Small drink of water from a cup

Bedtime   Breast-feed or 7–8 oz of formula

Feeding plan at eight to nine months

	Week 1	Week 2	Week 3	Week 4
Introduce	Butter	Cottage cheese	Brussels sprouts	Prunes
	Liver	Guava	Figs	Oranges
	Margarine	Celery	Tuna fish	Egg yolk

- Each day your baby should have three servings of carbohydrates, made up of cereal, whole grain bread, pasta or potatoes.
- He should have at least three portions of vegetables and fruit, including some raw chopped vegetables, and will need one portion of animal protein or two of vegetable protein.
- Vegetables and fruit with a high vitamin C content should be served with protein meals; this aids iron absorption.
- Figs and prunes should be washed thoroughly and soaked or stewed.
- Egg yolk can be introduced, but the egg should be hard-boiled.
- Choose tuna in olive oil, which has a lower salt content than water-packed.
- Your baby may show signs of wanting to feed himself. If so, use two spoons. Load one spoon for him to try and get the food into his mouth by himself and use the other spoon to actually get the food in. Help his coordination by holding his wrist and gently guiding him.
- By the end of nine months, a bottle-fed baby should be drinking all of his breakfast milk from a cup, but if he is losing interest in his milk, give him extra cheese, sauces or milk puddings.
- He still needs 18–20 oz of breast milk or formula a day, inclusive of milk used in sauces, puddings and cereals.
- By nine months his day's menu may look something like the following:

Breakfast Breast-feed or 6 oz of formula from a cup
Oat cereal with milk and fruit *or*
Whole grain cereal with milk and fruit *or*
Baby muesli with milk and fruit
Toast and butter or fruit spread

Lunch Braised liver, chopped cabbage and carrots *or*
Chicken with peach and pasta salad *or*

Lamb pot pie *or*
Tuna and egg yolk salad *or*
Chicken, broccoli and pasta in a cream sauce *or*
Fish cakes with brussels sprouts and lyonnaise potatoes
Fruit and yogurt
Drink of well-diluted juice from a cup

Dinner   Baked potato with grated cheese and apple *or*
Cheese and vegetable pizza *or*
Vegetable lasagne *or*
Carrot and lentil soup *plus*
Selection of finger sandwiches or rice crackers with a
savory spread
Cottage cheese with fruit or yogurt
Small drink of water from a cup

Bedtime   Breast-feed or 6–8 oz of formula

Feeding plan at nine to twelve months

	Week 1	Week 2	Week 3	Week 4
Introduce	Oily fish	Egg white	Dates	Beets
	Berries	Grapes	Eggplant	Cucumber
	Pineapple	Artichoke	Raisins*	Beef

* These should be offered to baby in small pieces, not whole, or soaked before serving.

- Your baby should be enjoying three well-balanced meals a day and be able to join in most of the family meals.
- During the final stage of weaning, the foods listed above should be introduced as and when you think your baby is ready. This will depend very much on how many teeth your baby has and how well he can chew.
- Each day your baby should have three to four servings of carbohydrates, made up of cereal, whole grain bread, pasta or potatoes.
- He should also have three to four portions of fruit and vegetables, including raw vegetables, and by the end of one year he should be used to raw salad vegetables.
- At this stage he should be eating lots of finger foods and nearly

all his fruit and vegetables should be chopped or sliced, instead of mashed.

- He will also need one portion of animal protein or two of vegetable protein.
- By the end of one year most meat, poultry and fish should be chopped up into small pieces instead of being minced or mashed.
- Different foods should not be all mixed together now. He will be much more aware of color and texture, so try to make his meals look interesting and appealing.
- Some babies will cut their 2:30 P.M. feed out altogether at this stage. If he is not taking 11½ oz between two feeds and inclusive of the milk used in his food, give him extra cheese and yogurt.
- By one year he still needs a minimum of 11½ oz a day of breast or formula milk, inclusive of milk used in cereal, sauces and puddings.
- Bottle-fed babies should be encouraged to take all of their breakfast milk from a cup. By the age of one year, you should also aim to replace the last bottle of formula with a drink from a cup.
- Cow's milk can be introduced as a drink from the age of one year; it should be full fat, pasteurized and preferably organic.
- By one year his day's menu may look something like the following:

Breakfast Breast-feed or a drink of formula milk from a cup
Whole grain or oat cereal with milk and fruit *or*
Baby muesli with milk and fruit *or*
Scrambled egg on toast
Toast with spread *plus*
Yogurt and chopped fruit

Lunch Cold, creamed chicken with apple and celery salad *or*
Beef meatballs in tomato sauce with pasta *or*
Tuna-burgers and mixed vegetables *or*
Irish stew with dumplings
Drink of water or well-diluted juice from a cup
Yogurt and fresh fruit

Mid-afternoon Drink of milk, water or well-diluted juice from
a cup

Dinner Thick soup and savory sandwiches *or*
Vegetarian pizza with green salad *or*

Chickpea and spinach croquettes with a homemade
tomato sauce *or*
Lentil and vegetable lasagne
Small drink of milk, water or well-diluted juice
from a cup

Bedtime   Breast-feed or 6 oz of formula from a cup

USEFUL ADDRESSES

American Academy of Pediatrics
141 Northwest Point Boulevard
Elk Grove Village, IL 60007-1098
Phone: (847) 228-5005
Fax: (847) 228-5097
Web address: www.aap.org

American College of Nurse-
Midwives
818 Connecticut Avenue NW,
Suite 900
Washington, DC 20006
Phone: (202) 728-9860
Fax: (202) 728-9897
Web address: www.midwife.org

American Massage Therapy
Association
820 Davies Street
Evanston, IL 60201
Phone: (847) 864-0123
Fax: (847) 864-1178
Web address:
www.amtamassage.org

La Leche League International
1400 N. Meacham Road
Schaumburg, IL 60173-4048
Phone: (847) 519-7730
Web address:
www.lalecheleague.org

Medela Inc.
P.O. Box 660
McHenry, IL 60051-0600
Phone: (800) 435-8316
Fax: (815) 363-9941
Web address: www.medela.com

Mothers & Others
40 West 20th Street
New York, NY 10011-4211
Web address: www.mothers.org

Sudden Infant Death Syndrome
Resource Center
2070 Chain Bridge Road, Suite 450
Vienna, VA 22182
Phone: (703) 821-8955
Fax: (703) 821-2098

Tiny Tummies
P.O. Box 2171
Sausalito, CA 94966-2171
Phone: (415) 206-9566
Web address: ttummies@aol.com

U.S. Consumer Product Safety
Commission
Washington, DC 20207
Phone: (800) 638-2772
Web address: www.cpsc.gov

The Vegetarian Resource Group
P.O. Box 1463
Baltimore, MD 21203
Phone: (410) 366-8343
Web address: www.vrg.org

FURTHER READING

American Academy of Pediatrics, et al., *Caring for Your Baby and Young Child: Birth to Age 5,* Bantam, 1998.

Brazelton, T. Berry, M.D., *Touchpoints: Your Child's Emotional and Behavioral Development,* Perseus Press, 1994.

Ferber, Richard, M.D., *Solve Your Child's Sleep Problems,* Simon & Schuster, 1986.

Gotsch, Gwen and Torgus, Judy, *The Womanly Art of Breastfeeding,* Plume, 1997.

Karmel, Annabel, *The Healthy Baby Meal Planner,* Fireside, 1992.

Leach, Penelope, *Your Baby and Child: From Birth to Age 5,* Knopf, 1997.

Neifert, Marianne, M.D., *Dr. Mom: A Guide to Baby and Child Care,* Signet, 1993

Sears, William, M.D., *Nighttime Parenting: How to Get Your Baby and Child to Sleep,* New American Library, 1987.

Stoppard, Dr. Miriam, *Complete Baby & Child Care,* DK Publishing, 1995.

Weissbluth, Marc, M.D., *Healthy Sleep Habits, Happy Baby,* Fawcett Books, 1999.

INDEX